Sigmund Freud

Jean-Michel Quinodoz introduces the essential life and work of Sigmund Freud, from the beginning of his clinical experiences in Vienna in the 1880s to his final years in London in the 1930s. Freud's discoveries, including universally-influential concepts like the Oedipus complex and the interpretation of dreams, continue to be applied in many disciplines today. Elegantly and clearly written, each chapter leaves the reader with a solid framework for understanding key Freudian concepts, and an appetite for further knowledge. Accessible for readers inside and outside the field of psychoanalysis, there is nothing at all equivalent in English.

The book starts with Freud's life before the discovery of psychoanalysis, spanning from 1856 to 1900, when *The Interpretation of Dreams* was published. The subsequent chapters are devoted to the presentation of the key notions of psychoanalysis. A chronological perspective shows how Freud's work has been constantly enriched by the successive contributions of Freud himself, as well as his successors. Freud's contributions are also embedded in the daily, clinical practice of psychoanalysis and psychotherapy. The last chapter concerns Freud's life from 1900 to 1939, the year of his death.

This fascinating, concise and accessible introduction to the life and work of Sigmund Freud, one of the most influential and revolutionary figures of the nineteenth and twentieth centuries, by internationally-renowned author Jean-Michel Quinodoz, will appeal to both professional readers and anyone with an interest in psychoanalysis, psychotherapy and the history of ideas. The book presents the major contributions of Sigmund Freud in their nascent state, as and when they appeared, and shows that they are as alive today as ever.

Jean-Michel Quinodoz is an internationally-acclaimed psychoanalytic theorist and clinician. He is author of *The Taming of Solitude, Dreams That Turn Over a Page, Reading Freud, Listening to Hanna Segal* and *Melanie Klein and Marcelle Spira* (all Routledge).

"*Sigmund Freud* is a book in which each chapter is a gem – a concise, very accessible rendering of the essence of Freud's psychoanalytic thinking, accessible by readers within and outside of the field of psychotherapy. This is not a textbook or primer; it is an insightful discussion of some of the most important ideas to be launched in the twentieth century." – **Dr. Thomas Ogden**, Psychoanalytic Institute of Northern California

"In his new, quite brief, book on Freud, Jean-Michel Quinodoz captures both the breadth and the depth of Freud's work. It is not a superficial summary of Freud's work, but rather a remarkable re-presentation and exploration of Freud's central psychoanalytic tenets that continue to underlie and inform our work today as psycho-analysts and psychotherapists." – **William F. Cornell**, author of *Explorations in Transactional Analysis*

"Jean-Michel Quinodoz is able to distil complex ideas into something easily available to a wide audience without talking down to his readers. He has managed to cover in this small book the main lines of Freud's oeuvre." – **Dr. Dana Birksted-Breen**, British Psychoanalytical Society and The Institute of Psychoanalysis

Sigmund Freud

An Introduction

Jean-Michel Quinodoz
Translated by Andrew Weller

Routledge
Taylor & Francis Group

LONDON AND NEW YORK

First published 2018
by Routledge
2 Park Square, Milton Park, Abingdon, Oxon OX14 4RN

and by Routledge
711 Third Avenue, New York, NY 10017

Routledge is an imprint of the Taylor & Francis Group, an informa business

This book is a translation of a work previously published in French as *Sigmund Freud* by Presses Universitaires de France in the series Que Sais-Je? (2015)

Translation into English by Andrew Weller

Trademark notice: Product or corporate names may be trademarks or registered trademarks, and are used only for identification and explanation without intent to infringe.

British Library Cataloguing in Publication Data
A catalogue record for this book is available from the British Library

Library of Congress Cataloging in Publication Data
Names: Quinodoz, Jean-Michel, author.
Title: Sigmund Freud : an introduction / Jean-Michel Quinodoz ; translated by Andrew Weller.
Other titles: Sigmund Freud. English
Description: Abingdon, Oxon ; New York, NY : Routledge, 2018. | Includes bibliographical references and index.
Identifiers: LCCN 2017002806 (print) | LCCN 2017018803 (ebook) | ISBN 9781315303918 (ebook) | ISBN 9781138235786 (hardback) | ISBN 9781138235793 (pbk.)
Subjects: LCSH: Freud, Sigmund, 1856-1939. | Psychoanalysts—Biography. | Psychoanalysis—History.
Classification: LCC BF109.F74 (ebook) | LCC BF109.F74 Q56313 2018 (print) | DDC 150.19/52092—dc23
LC record available at https://lccn.loc.gov/2017002806

ISBN: 978-1-138-23578-6 (hbk)
ISBN: 978-1-138-23579-3 (pbk)
ISBN: 978-1-315-30391-8 (ebk)

Typeset in Times New Roman
by Swales & Willis Ltd, Exeter, Devon, UK

Contents

Acknowledgements

I would like to address those who feel personally touched by reading Freud and who may be tempted by the experience of psychoanalysis or by a psychoanalytically-inspired approach. Drawing on my own personal experience of analysis, as well as on my practice of several decades as a clinical psychoanalyst, I can attest to the fact that psychoanalysis remains very much alive and that it is a therapeutic method that continues to offer a solution to the psychic suffering of many people.

I would like to express my thanks to Danielle, my first reader, and to my psychoanalytic readers Patricia Waltz, André Haynal and Juan Manzano, as well as to my friends Monique Küng, François Compagnon, and Piercarlo Righetti. I would like to express my thanks to my colleagues Patricia Waltz, André Haynal and Juan Manzano for their comments and suggestions, as well as to Andrew Weller for his excellent translation.

In Memory of Danielle

Introduction

A constantly evolving system of thought

The major contributions of Sigmund Freud are as alive today as in the past. When we discover them for ourselves, they have lost nothing of the freshness that they had when he described them for the first time. That is why I will present them in their nascent state, as and when they appeared.

This book is organised as follows. The first chapter is a reminder of Freud's life before the discovery of psychoanalysis, spanning the period from 1856, the year of his birth, to 1900, the date of the publication of *The Interpretation of Dreams* (1900). The following fourteen chapters are devoted to the presentation of the key notions of psychoanalysis, handed down by Freud to posterity. His psychoanalytic production spanned a period of almost fifty years and ended with his death in 1939. The last chapter concerns Freud's life from 1900 to 1939. In spite of the great interest of the historical context in which Freud developed his work, I thought it was important to separate his biography from the presentation of his ideas in order to give greater prominence to his psychoanalytic discoveries.

Far from being closed in on itself, his work remains an "open work," which has been constantly enriched thanks to the successive contributions of Freud himself and his successors. In the interests of clarity, I have decided not to mention these later developments. Moreover, I have used everyday words wherever possible, for Freud wrote in a plain and current form of the German language. I have also adopted a clinical perspective to emphasise that his thought, far from being pure speculation, is closely linked with the daily practice of the psychoanalytic treatment that it elucidates.

Freud's psychoanalytic work fills twenty or so volumes and his correspondence more than fifty. Apart from certain specialists, very few people succeed in acquiring an overview of it. Consequently, the way in which his ideas are understood varies in relation to many factors, among which are the reader's preferences, his/her life trajectory, his/her personal experience of psychoanalysis, or the translations he or she has chosen. Psychoanalysts, too, can understand Freud from different points of view, depending on the training they have received or the current of psychoanalytic thought to which they adhere. Each one has the tendency to prioritise aspects or periods of Freud's life and to conceal others.

It is difficult for a translator to reproduce the elegance of Freud's German writing without losing the clarity and precision with which he expresses his thinking. That is why numerous translations of his work exist, and all aim, in their own way, to stay as close as possible to the intention of the author.

Cologny (Geneva), 7 April 2015

Chapter 1

Sigmund Freud from 1856 to 1900[1]

1856. Freud was born on 6 May in Freiburg (now Priborg, in the Czech Republic). He was the son of Jakob, a Jewish merchant, and Amalia. In 1855, one year before Sigmund's birth, Jakob, who was twice widowed and already the father of two sons from a first marriage, got married for the third time, to Amalia. Seven other children followed the birth of Sigmund, two boys and five girls. Several significant elements of Sigmund Freud's childhood are worth noting. First, he was always able to rely on his self-confidence based on the certainty of being loved by Amalia, a mother who saw in her eldest son a great man of the future. Moreover, Sigmund found himself faced with the enigma posed by a confusing intergenerational situation within his own family. When he was born, his father was forty, Amalia was twenty, and his half-brother Philip, twenty-one. This situation could have led Sigmund to think that Philip was his mother's husband and that the "old" Jakob was his grandfather. Note that at the age of two, Sigmund lost his brother Julius, aged seven months, and that, shortly after, he was separated from his Nanny, a devout Catholic who had taken care of him until the age of 2½. **1860**. The family settled in Vienna. **1866**. When Sigmund was about ten years old, Jakob told him the story of a painful humiliation: once, in the street, Jakob had been obliged to pick up his fur hat which a passer-by, in an anti-Semitic gesture, had thrown into the gutter. This episode instilled in Sigmund a desire to reverse this humiliation by seeking to gain the respect of his contemporaries by virtue of his discoveries and his success for the rest of his life. The liberal socio-political atmosphere that pervaded Vienna at the time, especially in favour of the Jews, allowed Freud to envisage a better life than his father had known. He was to remain faithful to his Jewish origins, while at the same time defining himself as a "Jew without religion". **1873**. At the age of seventeen he received his "Matura" or secondary school diploma (equivalent to A-levels).

1874. Freud began medical studies at the Faculty of Medicine in Vienna. It was the beginning of the era of modernism, a movement which aimed to integrate and unify knowledge in all domains, thus opening up a dialogue between biology, medicine, the arts, literature and philosophy. Freud's thought was undoubtedly marked by the spirit of the times – the *Zeitgeist* – that reigned at that moment, especially in medicine, under the impetus of Professor Karl von Rokitansky. This eminent doctor introduced an integrated diagnostic approach, based both on the physical examination of the patient and on systematic scientific findings. Rokitansky's ideas spread beyond the faculty of medicine and influenced Viennese culture as a whole, from artists to laboratory researchers. The bases of modern thought in numerous disciplines were thus laid. Plunged into this stimulating environment, Sigmund developed a passionate interest for the exact sciences and launched his career as a scientific researcher. He harboured the ambition to become famous. He initiated himself into the theories of Darwin under the influence of Professor Carl Claus, Director of the Institute of Zoology. **1876**. He took up his post as an assistant to Professor Ernst Wilhelm von Brücke, Director of the Institute of Physiology, a representative of the positivist school and of biological determinism, and also Rokitansky's disciple. **1877**. Freud, aged twenty-one, visited Trieste. It was in this year that his first notable scientific publication, in which he confirmed the existence of testicles in the male eel, appeared. **1881**. Freud was twenty-five years old when he obtained the title of medical doctor. In Brücke's laboratory, he met Josef Breuer, a Viennese doctor, his elder by fourteen years, who had invented a "cathartic method" that made it possible to successfully treat hysterical patients, in particular, Anna O., the first case to receive this type of treatment. **1882**. Freud became an assistant at Vienna's General Hospital. There he met Theodor Nothnagel,

Professor of Internal Medicine, and then Theodor Meynert, head of the Psychiatric Hospital of Vienna, known for his work on brain anatomy and as a strict adherent of determinism. At the age of twenty-six, Freud met Martha Bernays, who was twenty and became his fiancée. During the following four years, they exchanged letters daily in which Freud showed himself to be a passionate, romantic, exclusive and even jealous lover. **1884**. Freud studied the pharmacological properties of cocaine on himself, but he missed out on the opportunity of seeing himself credited with the discovery of its effects in local anaesthetics. He pursued his studies on brain anatomy, aphasia and paralyses of infantile origin, before turning towards research in neurology, which was more promising. **1885**. Freud was named a *Privat Docent.* He obtained a grant for a six-month stay in Paris with Professor Jean-Martin Charcot, who fascinated him. Witnessing the induction and cure of hysterical paralyses simply by means of hysterical suggestion was to have a decisive influence on him. **1886**. Sigmund and Martha got married. The couple were to have six children between 1887 and 1896. Martha was a discreet, tender and efficient woman with her family, but was reserved with strangers: she presented herself as a housewife protecting her husband from the worries of everyday life. To earn his living, Sigmund gave up the idea of pursuing a career as a researcher, left his position at the hospital of Vienna and opened his own private practice. **1887**. He began corresponding with the Berlin physician Wilhelm Fliess, an otorhinolaryngologist who became the scientific confidant and personal friend whom Freud needed to share his discoveries, and this was the case until their separation in 1901. **1889**. Freud made a brief visit to Nancy to see Professor Hippolyte Bernheim, Charcot's rival, in order to improve his technique in hypnosis.

1890. At the age of thirty-four, Freud set up his private practice at home, at 19 Berggasse in Vienna, where he lived until his enforced exile to London in 1938. **1895**. Freud and Breuer published their *Studies on Hysteria* (1895); Freud's contribution is considered as being the beginning of psychoanalysis (see below, Chapter Two). **1896**. Shortly after the publication of *Studies on Hysteria,* Freud separated from Breuer to go his own way. The death of his father, Jakob, at the age of eighty-one, left him deeply distraught: he endured painful feelings of "survivor guilt". The same year, Minna Bernays, Martha's younger sister, took up residence in the apartment of her sister and her brother-in-law; the fact that she lived with the Freuds and even travelled to Italy with Sigmund gave rise to liaison rumours that were never proven. **1897**. Freud began his self-analysis, during which he studied his own dreams and discovered the mechanisms of dream-formation. During this self-analysis, he announced to Fliess that he had abandoned his theory of actual seduction as the sole cause of hysterical disorders and recognised the role played by seduction fantasies. In another letter to Fliess, Freud made for the first time a comparison between the incestuous and parricidal wishes felt in childhood and Sophocles' tragedy *Oedipus Rex.*

Note

1 For the period from 1900 to 1939, see Chapter Sixteen.

Chapter 2

Hysteria and the discovery of psychoanalysis

The first psychoanalytic publication

It is considered that Freud's contribution to *Studies on Hysteria*, a work published in collaboration with Josef Breuer, marked the birth of psychoanalysis as a method of treatment of psychic disorders, the prototype of which was hysteria. The work presents the clinical successes obtained by the two physicians during the previous fifteen years, as well as their respective hypotheses.

At the time, the term hysterical illness covered a series of varied somatic and psychic symptoms ranging from passing phenomena, such as convulsions or fainting fits to states of blindness or lasting paralyses. These symptoms did not involve anatomical or neurophysiological symptoms. Long considered as the expression of a specifically female illness, hysterical phenomena were very widespread at the end of the nineteenth century, although it was not possible to determine whether their origin was organic or psychic. Faced with this disconcerting symptomatology, the mainstream medical world tended to reject these patients – generally women – regarding them as mad or simply feigners. In the 1880s, a reputed Viennese physician, Josef Breuer, succeeded in treating hysterical patients by means of a method that he had invented, based on hypnosis. Hypnosis created a particular state that permitted the patient to get rid of her symptoms by reliving intensely every emotion associated with them, thereby producing an emotional discharge.

Breuer called it the "cathartic method" (from the Greek *catharsis,* "purification", "purgation"). In 1882, Breuer explained his method to Freud who applied it with similar success to his own patients. Stimulated by his spirit of investigation and the search for new discoveries, Freud perfected Breuer's technique and laid the foundations of what he was to call the psychoanalytic method.

From "catharsis" to the method of "free association"

In *Studies on Hysteria* (1895) Breuer described just one case, that of Anna O., whose treatment gained its place in history as the first of its kind. Aged twenty-one, the patient suffered from irrational anxieties, from variations of humour, disorders of language and vision, and a paralysis of the right side of her body. During the treatment, Breuer noticed that each time Anna O. reported a memory dating back to the moment when one of her symptoms had appeared for the first time and relived the emotions connected with it intensely, the symptom disappeared. To facilitate the return of the memory and the concomitant emotional discharge – or "abreaction" – Breuer resorted to hypnosis. In her own words, Anna O. described this treatment as a *talking cure* and the emotional discharge as *chimney sweeping.*

For his part, Freud wrote four clinical observations which show us how his technique was evolving:

(1) "Emmy von N." suffered from panic attacks and severe phobias, that is, from irrational fears, in particular at the sight of certain animals. With this patient, Freud began by applying Breuer's cathartic method in association with hypnosis. But in the course of the sessions, he noticed that all that was needed to produce the cathartic effect, without the help of hypnosis, was for the patient to tell him spontaneously about her significant memories. Freud concluded that henceforth he could let the patient express her thoughts freely, as the mere fact of expressing them verbally sufficed to obtain the desired effect.

(2) On the strength of this discovery, Freud made immediate and successful use of the "free association method" with "Miss Lucy R.", a young English governess for whom hypnosis did not work. He made a further step forward when he realised that the pathogenic effect of hysterical symptoms was due to a *repressed* idea, that is, an idea that is rejected because it is intolerable for the patient's conscious mind, and that the resulting intrapsychic conflict generally has a sexual content.

(3) The third success he had was with "Katarina", aged eighteen, during a walk they went on for several hours. This short treatment strengthened Freud's conviction that hysterical symptoms generally have their origin in a traumatic experience of a sexual nature and that their recollection permits the "abreaction" that is necessary to get rid of the symptom; in Katarina's case, it was the revival of a memory of an attempted seduction during her adolescence by her "uncle" – in reality by her own father – that turned out to be at the origin of the trauma.

(4) The observation of "Elizabeth von R." was the first complete analysis of a symptom of hysterical conversion. The patient suffered from violent pains in her legs and unclassifiable difficulties in walking until Freud made the diagnosis of hysterical conversion, according to which the physical disorders were the result of the transformation of a psychic conflict into a somatic symptom. The symptoms disappeared when the patient recalled an intolerable idea that she had "repressed" out of her conscious mind: when she was at the foot of the bed on which her dead sister was lying, she suddenly had the thought that she was now free to marry her brother-in-law. She had immediately pushed this idea out of her mind.

Laying the foundations of the psychoanalytic method

In his visionary theoretical chapter of the *Studies in Hysteria,* Freud went further than Breuer, whose explanation remained at the descriptive level. Indeed, Freud opened up new perspectives not only for treating hysteria, but also for understanding psychic functioning in general, thereby laying the theoretical and technical foundations of what was to become the psychoanalytic treatment.

He began by presenting the approach he had adopted once he had noticed that Breuer's cathartic method was very time-consuming and that hypnosis did not necessarily work with all patients. Rather than becoming disheartened, Freud overcame the obstacle by getting the patient to lie down and asking him to shut his eyes in order to concentrate. With his hands he sometimes applied a slight pressure to the patient's forehead so as to facilitate the emergence of new memories. But he also abandoned this technical gesture in favour of what he called the "method of free association", which remains today the "fundamental rule of psychoanalysis". This consists of asking the analysand, at the beginning of the treatment, to lie down on a couch, with the psychoanalyst sitting behind him, and to communicate his thoughts as they come spontaneously to his mind, without censoring them or seeking to order them in any way.

In spite of the successes obtained by this new approach, Freud often came up against obstacles that impeded the pathogenic ideas from emerging. He then had the idea that *resistances* and *defences* arise in the mind of the patient himself – a place that he was already calling the *ego*. For Freud, the aim of resistances was to *repress* irreconcilable ideas *out of the conscious mind* – into the *unconscious* – under the effect of a repressing force called *censorship*. Freud thus not only highlighted the fundamental elements of psychic functioning in general, such as the conscious, the unconscious and censorship, but also described for the first time the dynamic of repression and of the act of becoming conscious, a process that is still today the basis of the efficacy of the psychoanalytic method.

As for the mechanism of *conversion* often observed in hysterical patients, it results from the fact that emotion that has not been discharged exceeds the limits of what the patient can tolerate, in such a way that psychic energy *is converted* into somatic energy, alterating in the process a bodily function (aphasia, paralysed member, etc.). This observation by Freud on the psychic nature of the phenomenon of hysterical conversion accounts for the possible reversibility of this type of symptom and the possibility of eliminating it.

The role of the sexual factor

Freud noticed that the sexual factor played a decisive role when he realised that his patients – and not only his hysterical patients – frequently reported sexual traumas in their accounts of the appearance of their symptoms. The original trauma is always linked to sexual experiences that occurred in early childhood, before puberty, and which may be described as sexual abuses "in the strictest sense of the term", according to Freud. During a short period, between 1895 and 1897, he was persuaded that it could only be a question of real sexual experiences; although he had not yet mentioned the existence of "infantile sexuality", that is to say the fact that children present sexual impulses very early on. In the light of new observations, he made the hypothesis that a certain number of scenes reported by his patients as being *real facts* were in fact *imagined* rather than being real experiences. Henceforth, he considered that the traumatic factor determining the neuroses sometimes depended on a *real* experience and sometimes on a *fantasy*. Freud's hypothesis concerning the role of fantasy as a traumatic factor has given rise to many misunderstandings and is still the object of controversies today. However, let us recognise that when the practitioner has to face a situation of this kind, it is often extremely difficult for him to disentangle in the patient's discourse what belongs to reality and what to fantasy.

The symbolic determinism of hysterical symptoms

Freud also observed that hysterical symptoms have a meaning and that they are symbolically determined. The mechanism of symbolization is particularly striking in the phenomenon of conversion. Freud gave the example of a female patient who suffered from a sharp, stabbing pain between her eyes: when she told him that this pain reminded her of her grandmother's gaze which had "penetrated deeply into her forehead" (1895, p. 180), Freud noted that the pain had disappeared. This example shows not only that a symptom is symbolically determined, but also that speech – verbalization – allows an unconscious content to become conscious.

An outline of the notion of transference

Freud noted to begin with that the phenomenon of transference is the essential work, but he then considered it as an obstacle to becoming aware of resistances. The obstacle stems from the fact that the patient expresses expectations towards the physician which he cannot respond to for the reason that they are not in fact addressed to him. But the patient is not aware of this. Freud reported the case of a female patient who wanted a man she knew to take her in his arms and kiss her. At the end of a session, she was overtaken by the same desire for Freud, which filled her with horror. Once she had reported to him the content of this resistance, it was overcome and the work could continue. Freud described this phenomenon is a *mésalliance* or a *false connection:* "Since I have discovered this, I have been able, whenever I have been similarly involved personally, to presume that a transference and a false connection have once more taken place. Strangely enough, the patient is deceived afresh each time this is repeated" (1895, p. 303). Later on, Freud would make this "displacement" of pathogenic ideas the best ally of the psychoanalyst's work (see Chapter Eight).

Chapter 3

Self-analysis

In Freud's private sphere: his letters to Wilhelm Fliess

Between 1895 and 1900 Freud saw his initial hypotheses confirmed with his patients. His new observations enabled him to publish several articles in which he applied to other neuroses – phobic and obsessional – the same sexual origin that he had postulated for hysteria. But the essential part of his scientific work took place outside the domain of publication, in an inner development which we would never have known about if it had not been for the discovery of the letters that he wrote to his friend, the Berlin physician Wilhelm Fliess, between 1887 and 1904. These letters were acquired in 1936 from a Viennese antiquary by Marie Bonaparte, one of his first French disciples, and were made public partially in 1950 and in totality in 1985 (Freud, 1887–1904). Their major interest resides in the fact that this correspondence allows us to follow the self-analysis that Freud undertook between 1896 and 1899, and to observe two fundamental turning-points in his thinking: he gave up his theory of actual seduction in favour of the fantasy of seduction and abandoned the idea of basing psychoanalysis on the exact sciences.

Real seduction, fantasy of seduction

In the course of reading the letters to his friend Wilhelm Fliess, we realise that Freud was beginning to doubt the reality of the scenes of seduction that his female patients reported to him so frequently. Calling into question his hypothesis of the origin of neurosis founded exclusively on a theory of *actual* seduction, he gradually acquired the conviction that *fantasies* of seduction – the fruit of a heightened imagination – can have the same traumatic effect as *actual* scenes of seduction; "I no longer believe in my *neurotica*," he wrote to Fliess, speaking about his initial theory of real seduction (letter dated 21 September 1897 in Freud, 1887–1904, p. 264). How can we explain that sexual fantasies born of the imagination can have the same traumatic power as a real seduction? For Freud, the explanation lay in the existence of what he called "infantile sexuality", a notion he would develop shortly afterwards in his *Three Essays on the Theory of Sexuality* (1905b). In effect, children also experience emotions, sensations and sexual thoughts; and we know only too well how it is often difficult for them to distinguish between reality and fantasy. In the case of neurosis, adults regress to an infantile stage in which this distinction between what is real and what is imaginary tends to become blurred. Clinically, this distinction still remains difficult to establish today, not only for the patient himself but also for those around him, and even for the psychoanalyst. It is worth noting that, although Freud had given up his initial theory, he continued to affirm throughout his life that actual scenes of seduction can also provoke pathogenic effects.

Self-analysis and the discovery of the Oedipus complex

Shortly after his father's death in 1896, Freud began what he called his self-analysis, focusing essentially on the analysis of his dreams. Thanks to this work of introspection, which he continued until 1899, he discovered the role played by dreams in his psychic life as well as the importance of infantile sexuality in his own childhood. Thus in a letter to Fliess, he reports his recollection of the early awakening of his libido: "[I discovered too] that, later on, (between the ages of two and two-and-a-half) my libido was awakened towards *matrem*,[1] and this was on the occasion of a trip I made with her from Leipzig to Vienna, during which we must have spent a night together, and where I certainly had the opportunity of seeing her *nudam*"[2] (letter dated 3 October, 1897 in Freud, 1887–1904, p. 268). In another letter to Fliess, Freud mentions the feelings of love he had for his mother and his jealousy towards his father, and he associates them for the first time with Sophocle's tragedy, *Oedipus Rex,* ten years before he introduced the notion of the Oedipus complex as a fundamental concept of psychoanalysis (see Chapter Seven). Note that in this letter Freud only mentions the "direct" form of the Oedipus complex as it appears in the boy who wishes to usurp his father's place with his mother. He was to describe several other forms later on.

Generally speaking, Freud's work is teeming with judicious observations which often prove to be highly significant *a posteriori* from a psychoanalytic point of view. Nonetheless, the time that elapses between the moment Freud notes an observation and the moment he attributes to the phenomenon observed a specific function that deserves a specific designation in the field of psychoanalysis is variable. This is the case for many notions, such as that of censorship, which was mentioned for the first time in the *Studies on Hysteria* in 1895, but took nearly thirty years to acquire the status of a psychoanalytic concept under the term *superego* (see Chapter Twelve).

Psychoanalysis does not belong to the exact sciences

A copy of one of Freud's manuscripts entitled *Project for a Scientific Psychology* (1950 [1895]), was found among the letters sent to his friend Fliess. This text was not intended for publication because Freud had destroyed the original. It is a precious document on several counts. First, it marked a major turning-point in Freud's evolution from the moment he had abandoned the idea of founding psychoanalysis on quantifiable scientific facts. It is worth recalling that he possessed a solid training as an investigator, and that he retained the idea throughout his life that advances in biology and neuroscience would make it possible one day to better elucidate psychic functioning as conceived by psychoanalysis.

Thus, shortly after the discovery in 1892 of neurons and synaptic transmissions, Freud attempted to draw a comparison between neurophysiological mechanisms and psychic phenomena as he observed them in the neuroses. Soon realising that this attempt led to an impasse, he changed course and established psychoanalysis in its own field.

In the same unfinished manuscript, Freud turned towards the study of various instinctual processes and examined them in the light of his conception of psychic functioning. For example, he tried to account for the psychobiological phenomena triggered by hunger in the young infant and by sexual desire in the adult by resorting to psychological notions such as those of satisfaction and dissatisfaction, pleasure and unpleasure, love and hate, relations between people, and so on. These investigations heralded new developments that would appear in the *Metapsychological Papers* (1915–1917) (see Chapter Ten).

Notes

1 Mother, in Latin.
2 Nude, in Latin.

Chapter 4

The interpretation of dreams

The interpretation of dreams
is the royal road to knowledge of the
unconscious activities of the mind

(Freud, 1900, p. 608)

A revolutionary work

Of all his works, Freud considered that the most important was *The Interpretation of Dreams*, which appeared in 1900. Indeed, the entirely new ideas that he presented in it turned the hitherto accumulated corpus of knowledge on the subject upside down. He defends the idea that the dream is an organised psychic activity, specific to the dreamer, which is different from that of waking life and possesses its own laws. Beyond the dream itself, his revolutionary ideas shed new light on the functioning of thought and language. Freud thus distanced himself from the conception arising from Antiquity according to which dreams are symbolic premonitory messages sent by higher powers. He also distanced himself from the science of his time which saw them as a disorganised neurophysiological production, without psychological significance.

Dreams have a meaning

Freud turned his interest towards the scientific study of dreams from the moment he understood that hysterical symptoms had a meaning.

By applying his method of free association to his patients, he observed that the account of their dreams revealed the origin of hysterical symptoms in the same way as their associative discourse. This finding enabled him to establish connections between dreams, free associations, and the symbolic significance of symptoms. Freud grasped the significance, then, of the role played by dream life not only in psychopathology, but also in normal psychic functioning.

It took Freud four years, from 1895 to 1899, to write *The Interpretation of Dreams* (1900). During this period, Freud analysed his own dreams, which contributed to a large extent to the development of his hypotheses. The theme of the death of his father, Jakob Freud, in 1896, as well as many memories connected with him, appeared recurrently in his dreams and was the ferment of his self-analysis. This was a difficult period, and we may suppose that Freud wrote this book not only for scientific purposes but also in an attempt to overcome the inner crisis into which this bereavement had plunged him. This experience was nonetheless fruitful, for it was through his self-analysis and by interpreting his own dreams that Freud developed the specific psychoanalytic technique of interpretation.

The full edition contains more than 700 pages. Within it, Freud analyses almost 200 dreams, forty-seven of which are his own, and the others coming from his close acquaintances or colleagues. The study of dreams was an ongoing concern of Freud's throughout his life. In later editions he made alterations/modifications to the book. Although this work is an inspired book, its complexity makes it difficult to read. That is why its publisher asked Freud to write a summarized version, for didactic purposes, with the title *On Dreams* (1901a).

Fundamental principles of the interpretation of dreams

Before interpreting the proper content of a dream, Freud invites us always to take into account four principles. When a patient reports a dream, we must distinguish between the *manifest content,* that is to say the dream as reported by the dreamer, whose meaning is generally obscure, and the *latent content* which only emerges clearly after being deciphered in the light of the patient's associations. Indeed, one cannot understand the content of a dream taken in isolation, without asking the dreamer to communicate the thoughts that come to his/her mind when applying the method of free association. In the absence of the *dreamer's associations*, the therapist is sometimes tempted to bring his/her own associations, at the risk of interfering with the patient's thoughts. Finally, the dream scenario is regularly organised around *day residues*, events of the previous day of which the dream content retains a trace. These day residues are more or less closely related to the unconscious wish that is fulfilled in the dream.

On the basis of these elements, the psychoanalyst looks for the repressed *unconscious wish* that is fulfilled in the dream: "A dream," Freud writes, "is the (*disguised*) fulfilment of a (*suppressed or repressed*) wish" (1900, p. 160). In children, the underlying wish is generally clear, like that of the little girl who dreams of the strawberries that she had not been allowed to eat the day before. Generally speaking, with adults, the dream content seems incoherent because the *dream-work* has transformed the dream-thoughts in such a way that the fulfilled wish does not appear in the dream narrative and remains repressed. It is then the task of the *work of analysis* to perform the reverse operation to rediscover the latent, unconscious meaning of the dream-thoughts. "The task of dream interpretation," Freud writes, "is to unravel what the dream-work has woven" (1901a, p. 686). Freud adds that it is generally erotic wishes that are repressed, but not always, and that these wishes have their origin in infantile sexuality.

Five unconscious mechanisms for disguising the content of a dream

The *dream-work* uses the following techniques with the aim of disguising the unconscious thoughts of the dream.

Condensation consists in bringing together and compressing into a single unit dissimilar fragments belonging to different associative trains of thought. As the analysis of a dream progresses, we observe that dreams are "overdetermined", that is to say each of the dream fragments is derived in its turn from a series of elements that are themselves dissimilar, even though they are unconsciously linked to one another. Condensation is one of the fundamental mechanisms of the dream-work, but this procedure is also present in the formation of symptoms, slips of the tongue, bungled actions, and jokes.

Through *displacement,* the dream-work replaces the most significant thoughts of the dream by incidental thoughts. In this way, the fulfilment of a wish is decentred, in such a way that we lose all trace of it. Condensation and displacement are often associated at the heart of "compromises".

The *procedure of representation or representability*[1] is the means by which the dream-work succeeds in transforming thoughts into visual images. This method, associated with condensation and displacement, is comparable to the art of the caricaturist who succeeds in illustrating an idea by bringing together incongruous elements in one and the same drawing.

Secondary elaboration consists in presenting dream-content in the form of a coherent and intelligible scenario. But this coherence is merely apparent, for it is equally the result of a process of disguise aimed at concealing the fulfilment of an unconscious wish.

Dramatization is the fifth mechanism; it involves the process of transforming a thought by placing it in a dramatic context, a procedure that is similar to that of the stage director who takes a text in prose as a starting-point for creating a scenario and dialogues for a play or a film.

Censorship and repression

For Freud, the chief reason for distortion in dreams lies in censorship, which was subsequently called the *superego*. Its role is to allow dream-contents that it tolerates to pass into consciousness and to repress intolerable contents into the unconscious. But repression is never complete, so that derivatives of the repressed unconscious can well up again into consciousness: they then appear in the form of "compromises" – in particular in the form of symptoms – that have been distorted by condensation and displacement, mechanisms that allowed them to evade censorship.

The role of symbolism in dreams

The creation of symbols plays a primordial role in dream-formation. Dreams appear first and foremost in the form of visual images, less frequently in the form of verbal, auditory or sensory images. The essential aim of symbols consists in stripping the sexual images of their intelligibility in order to deceive the censorship. Freud distinguishes between two kinds of symbolism: universal symbolism and individual symbolism. He thought at first that dreams drew their material from universal symbolism derived from a remote past; but he realised that this was a reductive point of view which gave rise to arbitrary interpretations, far removed from the thoughts of the dreamer. With experience, he observed that each symbol can have a variety of meanings and that in addition to a universal symbolism, there exists an individual symbolism, specific to the dreamer, which appears when one turns to the dreamer's free associations. In clinical practice, Freud recommends the use of a dual approach which takes account of both the universal and the individual aspects of symbolism.

The technique of interpreting dreams

Based on the detailed analysis of a dream that is now famous, "Irma's injection", Freud illustrates his theses by describing the method of interpreting dreams which he developed during his self-analysis. First, he carefully notes down the material of the dream as reported by the dreamer on waking up; he then breaks it down into several elements; then he makes a note of the associations which arise freely in relation to each fragment of the dream; and finally, he establishes links between the different sequences which will form the basis for possible interpretations of the dream. I refer the reader to the two dreams that Freud analyses in painstaking detail: "Irma's injection" (1900, pp.106–120) and the "Table d'hôte" (1901a, pp. 636–641).

A theory of mental functioning

At the end of *The Interpretation of Dreams*, in light of his clinical observations on dreams and in neurotics, Freud offers a general view of the functioning of the psychic apparatus. He deliberately abandons the field of neurophysiology and puts forward a theoretical model of the mind in which he locates the unconscious, the preconscious, and the conscious. Freud calls this virtual model a "topographical point of view", with reference to the topographical localizations within the mind. On this basis, he examines the way in which these different places in the mind are related to each other and clarifies the role played by censorship in the mechanism of repression and the formation of dreams. In mental functioning, he also establishes a distinction between primary and secondary processes. Primary processes are characterised by an intolerance of frustration and the need for immediate satisfaction; they predominate in psychopathology. As for secondary processes, they exercise a regulatory function over the former thanks to the intervention of the *ego*, an agency capable of tolerating frustration, inhibiting immediate discharge, and deferring satisfaction. He was to complete his views in 1915 in the *Papers on Metapsychology* (see Chapter Ten).

Note

1 Translator's note: in German, *Darstellbarkeit*.

Chapter 5

Manifestations of the unconscious in everyday life

In publishing *The Psychopathology of Everyday Life* (1901b) and *Jokes and their Relation to the Unconscious* (1905a), Freud wanted to provide for the public at large irrefutable evidence of the existence of the unconscious in everyday life, as it manifests itself through the "failures" of repression that are parapraxes and jokes (*Witz* in German). He shows that the underlying psychic mechanism is not different from that which we find at the origin of dreams or in the production of symptoms. The difference between neurosis and normality is a question of proportion.

The Psychopathology of Everyday Life (1901b): slips of the tongue and parapraxes

What is a parapraxis?

It is an unintentional error or slip that can occur in the life of every normal individual, and not only in a neurotic. In the German language, the concept of parapraxis (*Fehlleistung*) has a wide meaning; it includes a vast range of apparently trivial phenomena such as involuntary gestures, slips of the tongue, acts of forgetting, negations or mistakes which are not limited to actual acts. Furthermore, in the German language, all these failures of the unconscious are preceded by the prefix *ver-*, which has the advantage of giving them a common denominator: "*das Vergessen* (forgetting), *das Versprechen* (slip of the tongue), *das Verlesen* (misreading), *das Verschreiben* (slips of the pen), *das Vergreifen* (bungled action), *das Verlieren* (mislaying)" (Laplanche & Pontalis, 1967, pp. 300–301). Among the many examples of parapraxes given by Freud, I shall choose the following: it concerns the President of the Lower House of the Austrian Parliament who had ceremoniously opened the sitting by declaring it *closed*, a mistake that gave rise to general merriment. For Freud, such a disturbance of language is the result of a compromise between a *conscious* intention of the President – to "open" the sitting – and an aggressive, *unconscious* wish that accompanies it – to "close" the sitting" – which prevailed in his actual discourse.

It is rare for an author of a failure of the unconscious to be able to grasp the significance of it right away, for these manifestations of the unconscious are subject to many inner resistances which impede their illumination. Notwithstanding their variety, these manifestations express an idea or wish that is intolerable for the conscious mind. They have undergone repression and yet return to consciousness after having been rendered unrecognisable in order to evade censorship. The methods of disguise used are similar to those operative the dreamwork: condensation, displacement, substitution, etc. As in the analysis of a dream or symptom, it is by resorting to free association that the hidden meaning of a parapraxis can be discovered.

The dynamic unconscious

The notion of unconscious in Freud's work calls for comment. The existence of the unconscious was known well before Freud, but not in the dynamic sense in which he understands it. Indeed, since the philosophers of Antiquity and probably well before that, it had been recognized that a large part of our mental activity occurs without our knowing it, so the idea of an unconscious was already present. But the unconscious of which Freud speaks is indissoluble from this repression: by unconscious he means a virtual psychic place to which ideas that are incompatible for the conscious mind are relegated, thereby escaping consciousness. It is a "dynamic unconscious", to be distinguished from the unconscious in general.

Jokes and their Relation to the Unconscious (1905a): the comic effect of jokes

Freud makes a general survey here of the various forms of comic situations included under the term jokes. Freud's attention had been drawn to them by Wilhelm Fliess who, when reading the proofs of *The Interpretation of Dreams*, had noted that puns occurred frequently in dreams. Freud's interest was not only scientific. He himself was a man full of wit, collecting puns and sprinkling his correspondence with humoristic anecdotes. He was fond of Jewish stories, but especially those told by Jews themselves, for "they know their real faults as well as the connection between them and their good qualities, and the share which the subject has in the person found fault with creates the subjective determinant of the joke-work" (1905a, pp. 111–112).

The comic effect of the joke is obtained by two distinct techniques: the first is based on words themselves and depends on verbal expression; and the second is based on the thought contained in the joke, which is itself independent of the wording in which it is expressed.

Techniques based on words

Freud differentiates three distinct technical methods which all use condensation, a characteristic mechanism of the dream-work: (a) The first method consists in condensing two words or two fragments of words in such a way as to create a neologism which, at first sight, is absurd, but which has a comic meaning for those listening to it. For example, Freud cites the joke of "Cleopold" created by those who made fun of an ill-matched couple by condensing the name of the prince – "Leopold" – and that of a lady – "Cleo". (b) The second method consists in using a single word, but giving it a double meaning. Freud gives an example based on the homophony between the name "Rousseau" and the words *roux* (red-haired) and *sot* (*silly*). Here the technique of the joke lies in the fact that one and the same word – "Rousseau" – is used in it in two ways, once as a whole, and again divided up into its separate syllables, like a charade. (c) The third method used by the joke consists in using the double meaning of a word or the multiple senses of one and the same word, as it is used in puns or "plays upon words", which Freud considers as the ideal case of the multiple use of the same material. According to him, it is the economy of means that governs the formation of the condensation in the three techniques.

Techniques based on thought

Jokes based on *thought* do not reside in the joke itself, but in the process of thought, and are independent of the form of expression. In these cases the *joke-work* – as he calls it by analogy with the dream-work – makes use of thought-processes that deviate from normal reasoning for producing a joking form of expression. He cites several methods, for example, that of *displacement* which uses logic to cover over faulty reasoning, or again the method that uses *nonsense* to produce a joke. The technique here involves saying something stupid, something absurd, which has the aim of exposing something else that is stupid or absurd. Freud gives an example. "Two Jews met in a railway carriage at a station in Galicia. 'Where are you going?' asked one. 'To Cracow', was the answer. 'What a liar you are!' broke out the other. 'If you say you're going to Cracow, you want me to believe you're going to Lemberg. But I know that in fact you're going to Cracow. So why are you lying to me?'" Freud stresses that the absurdity here is associated with a representation by the opposite, "for, according to the uncontradicted assertion of the first Jew, the second is lying when he tells the truth and is telling the truth by means of a lie" (1905a, p. 115).

Chapter 6

Infantile sexuality

In his *Three Essays on the Theory of Sexuality* (1905b), Freud openly challenges the prejudices of his time concerning sexuality. In simple everyday language, he puts forward a certain number of revolutionary ideas, while broadening the notion of sexuality and showing that it has its origin in early childhood. And yet he revealed nothing that was not already familiar to parents, educators or writers who, since time immemorial, had already observed and described the manifestations of infantile sexuality. The publication of this book gave the impression that Freud was of an obscene and pansexualist turn of mind. It was to damage his relations with the public for quite some time to come.

Sexual deviations: disturbances of infantile psychosexual development

Before tackling the description of normal infantile sexuality, Freud begins with psychopathology. He shows that sexual deviations have their origin in early childhood and result from a disturbance of psychosexual development. This was innovative in comparison with the scientists of his time for whom these deviations were the result of constitutional or innate degeneracy.

Freud distinguishes between two types of sexual deviation. The first type consists in a deviation in respect of the sexual *object*,[1] (i.e. in respect of the person who is felt to be sexually attractive). This is the case, for instance, with homosexuality, where the object of the sexual drive is a person of the same sex. What determines such an object-choice psychologically? For Freud, this choice is based on the existence of psychological bisexuality, a notion introduced by his friend Wilhelm Fliess. Freud's innovative views explain the coexistence of male and female tendencies within the same individual, so that the final object-choice depends on factors linked to infantile development.

The second type of sexual deviation is based on the notion of *part-drive* and *erogenous zone*. This type consists in a deviation in respect of the sexual *aim* (i.e. regarding the act towards which the drive tends). In these situations, the sexual drive is broken down into different components which he calls part-drives, and which have their source of excitation in a bodily zone known as an "erogenous zone". Among these deviations, some use parts of the body or fetishist objects as a means of obtaining sexual satisfaction. This type of deviation replaces the bodily zones which are normally meant for sexual intercourse. Others are based on fixations to the phase of preliminary erotic pleasure and are linked to the different erogenous zones such as the mouth (fellation, cunnilingus), to looking (voyeurism), touching, sadism or masochism. The presence of these fixations leads to disturbances at the level of genital sexuality.

By arguing that the predisposition to perversions is by no means exceptional but rather a part of the so-called normal constitution, already outlined in childhood, Freud particularly shocked the general public and gave rise to a lasting misunderstanding.

Normal infantile sexuality

Until then, scientists, along with the general public, thought that the sexual drive was absent in the child. But Freud innovated by attributing this ignorance to what he calls *infantile amnesia* (i.e. to the fact that adults have very few memories of their earliest childhood years). For Freud, infantile amnesia results from normal repression, depending on a mechanism similar to that which is operative in hysteria. In the child, manifestations of sexuality are already apparent in early childhood and are masturbatory in nature. Freud distinguishes three phases of infantile masturbation: the first is linked to the pleasure experienced by the infant at the breast-feeding stage; the second coincides with the height of the Oedipus complex around the third or fourth year; and the third corresponds to pubertal masturbation, which for a long time was the only kind taken into account.

Infantile sexual theories

Infantile sexuality manifests itself in a particularly explicit way through the unrelenting questions children ask on the subject of adult sexuality, questions that are an expression of the intense sexual curiosity that inhabits them from an early age. Where do babies come from? What do mummy and daddy do in bed? Do women also have a "widdler"? How do babies come out?

Under the name of "infantile sexual theories", Freud includes the multiple hypotheses that children toy with before acquiring a real knowledge of adult sexuality. These more or less conscious fantasy constructions do not disappear completely, and traces of them can frequently be found in the unconscious of adults.

Stages of development

In the *Three Essays on the Theory of Sexuality,* Freud introduces the notion of stages of psychosexual development. Infantile development goes through a certain number of phases, each of which is characterised by the primacy of a given erotic zone and of a particular mode of object-relating: Freud calls them the oral, sadistic-anal, phallic and genital stages. This evolution is, however, not linear and many overlappings occur, with each stage leaving permanent traces behind it.

The oral stage

This appears during the first months of life and is organised around the erogenous zone of the mouth and lips which has the function of absorbing. On the basis of this bodily function, the sensory pleasure of sucking the mother's breast is established through analysis; it is a prelude to maternal love, which allows Freud to assert that "a child sucking at his mother's breast has become the prototype of every relation of love" (1905b, p. 222). From this point of view, a fixation at the level of the oral erogenous zone may give rise to a greedy character, a tendency that becomes pathological in addictions and certain forms of psychosis.

The sadistic-anal stage

This stage occurs during the second year around the anal erogenous zone and the bowel function. The biological functions of the evacuation and retention of stools are at the basis of a psychological conflict dominated by control/rejection or opposition/submission in the relations with persons in the immediate family circle. The difference between the sexes is not yet established: "At the stage of the sadistic-anal organisation there is as yet no question of male and female; the antithesis between active and passive is the dominant one (1923b, p. 145). A fixation at the level of the sadistic-anal erogenous zone determines, for example, an obstinate, meticulous character, traits that can be found in a pathological mode in obsessional neurosis.

The phallic stage

The phallic stage appears in boys and girls between the ages of three and four, following the previous stages. During this period, which coincides with the height of the Oedipus complex, the child becomes aware of the difference between the sexes but, for Freud, he or she thinks of it solely in relation to the possession of the penis. Indeed, according to Freud neither the boy nor the girl has as yet a perception of the existence of female genital organs: "At the following stage, that of the infantile genital organisation, maleness exists but not femaleness; the antithesis here is between having a male genital organ and being castrated" (Freud, 1923b, p. 145). Thus for Freud the difference between the sexes is organised around the possession or privation of the penis at the anatomical level, and also depends on the antithesis, at the level of fantasy, between phallic and castrated; the phallus representing symbolically the omnipotence of the male organ.

In the boy, the appearance of the phallic stage corresponds to the increase of excitation felt at the level of his penis, the erogenous organ of this stage, and to the simultaneous emergence of unlimited wishes for omnipotence, symbolised by the phallus at the level of fantasy. In this context, namely, that of the Oedipus complex, the boy will be confronted by castration anxiety which governs its resolution.

The girl also goes through a phallic stage. According to Freud, her psychosexual development is also centred on the primacy of the penis as the sole determining erogenous zone. At this stage, the girl experiences "penis envy" and suffers from a complex of castration (a complex and not castration-anxiety, because she cannot experience anxiety to do with losing an organ that she does not have). Her Oedipus complex is resolved when the wish for a child replaces penis-envy owing to the symbolic equivalence "penis = child".

Freud was to persist in his belief in the primacy of the male organ during the psychosexual development of boys and girls, in spite of the protests voiced by women psychoanalysts in particular. There is reason to be surprised, however, that he minimised the role played by early perception of the female organs in the constitution of psychosexual identity. Indeed, in the case of the analysis of Little Hans (1909a), he had himself expressed the possibility that the child had perceived the existence of the vagina at a very early age, but he never integrated these observations into his theoretical conceptualisation (see Chapter Nine). Finally, it should be noted that the primacy that Freud gave to the penis in relation to psychosexual development is only a partial aspect of the development of boys and girls: it is essentially an infantile sexual theory that has to be overcome to gain access to adult genital sexuality. Moreover, Freud himself recognised that his knowledge concerning female sexuality was sketchy and he left it to his successors to explore the question more fully. It was the task of post-Freudian psychoanalysts to complete his views by giving a positive psychoanalytic description of femininity, one that was not simply based on a lack.

The polymorphously perverse predisposition

The discovery of the early role played by the erogenous zones led Freud to consider that there exists in the infant what he calls a *polymorphously perverse predisposition,* a notion that is still often poorly understood. What does it mean? This term means that the different parts of the body of the young child present, from the very beginnings of life, a particularly strong sensitivity to eroticization; it is only later that the erogenous zones are subjected to the genital organisation which aims to orient and unify sexuality. As for the term "polymorphously", he emphasises the great diversity of the erogenous zones that are liable, in the child, to be aroused by excitation at an early age. This hypersensibility explains why sexual abuses have such devastating effects on a child, because the premature excitation of erogenous zones creates fixations which disorganise subsequent development and have repercussions right into adult life by impeding the integration of the component sexual drives which guarantee the full development of genital maturity.

The notion of polymorphously perverse infantile predisposition should not be confused with that of perversion in the adult, as is sometimes the case. Adult perversion consists in a highly organised form of behaviour in which component satisfaction is obtained to the detriment of the full development of the individual's genital sexuality. Sexual pleasure is obtained by demanding particular conditions, as in fetishism.

The genital stage

The genital stage begins in puberty, a period during which the child really acquires a faculty for perception that marks the transition from the pre-genital stages towards adult sexuality. "It is not until development has reached its completion at puberty," Freud writes, "that the sexual polarity coincides with male and female ... the vagina becomes valued as an asylum for the penis, it comes into the inheritance of the mother's womb" (1923b, p. 145). It was now, too, that Freud described infantile development in terms of object-relations and elaborated the progressive transition from the *auto-eroticism* of early childhood, linked to masturbation and narcissism, towards the postpubertal *object-choice,* the moment when one person is chosen as love-object. He thus distinguishes between the choice of a *part* object and the choice of a *whole* object.

The choice of a part-object characterises the early stages of infantile development. The term *part* means, for example, that the mother's breast is seen by the infant as representing his mother entirely, the part being taken for the whole. The infant does not in fact see her yet as a *whole* person, which is, as a mother synthesizing the different aspects of his person, the whole being a synthesis of the different parts. This slow evolution pursues its course until puberty, during which a progressive integration of the component drives takes places leading to the object-choice that is described as *whole,* characterizing the genital stage.

Simultaneously, Freud was to give greater consideration to the role played by the affects of love and hate. He distinguishes between an *affectionate* affective current, which predominates in the pre-genital stages of the component drives, and a *sensual* affective current which is characteristic of a whole object-choice at the post-pubertal genital stage. The new object-choices remain influenced by the early choices, so that none of us escapes the influence of the first incestuous object-choices of infancy which will persist throughout life: "Even a person who has been fortunate enough to avoid an incestuous fixation of his libido does not entirely escape its influence" (1905b, p. 228).

Note

1 It is worth pointing out that psychoanalysis uses the term "object" in the classical sense for referring not to a thing, but to a person: "the object of my desire"; the object of my anger", etc.

Chapter 7

The Oedipus complex and the unconscious

The most famous legacy left by Freud, namely, the Oedipus complex, appears in the course of the child's development and is the central organiser of psychic life around which the individual's sexual identity is structured. This complex is held to be universal: "Every new arrival on the planet is faced with the task of mastering the Oedipus complex; anyone who fails to do so falls a victim to neurosis" (1905b, p. 226, note 1 added in 1920). This complex does not only concern the development of the normal individual, but is also present at the heart of psychopathology and forms, according to Freud, "the nucleus of neurosis".

Incestuous and parricidal wishes

As we saw earlier, it was during his self-analysis that Freud was led to recognise the love that he felt for his mother and the rivalry that set him in opposition to his father in his childhood. He linked this conflict of feelings to the Oedipal myth. The theme was taken up again in *The Interpretation of Dreams*: "King Oedipus, who slew his father Laïus and married his mother Jocasta, merely shows us the fulfilment of our own childhood wishes" (1900, p. 262) We have almost all, at one time or another, heard a little boy exclaiming, towards the age of three or four: "Later, I will marry Mummy, we don't need Daddy any more!" or a little girl, saying: "I want to live with Daddy, Mummy can go away!"

It was in 1910 that the term "Oedipus complex" appeared for the first time as a specific psychoanalytic concept in Freud's work, the notion of complex coming from Jung.

The Oedipal myth and the unconscious

Freud established from the outset a connection between the feelings that he had during his childhood and the scenario of Sophocles' *Oedipus Rex*. I will summarize briefly here the myth as it was revealed to Oedipus, the hero of this tragedy, during a series of *a posteriori* revelations that form the scenario. Let us look at it with fresh eyes.

Following a terrifying oracle, the King of Thebes, Laïus, and his wife Jocasta, felt threatened by the birth of a son, Oedipus, and left him to die on a mountainside. But the infant was found and brought up by King Polybus of Corinth and his wife, Queen Merope. The oracle had predicted that Oedipus would kill his father and marry his mother. On learning this when he was an adult, Oedipus fled Corinth to avoid killing Polybus and Merope, not knowing that they were foster parents and not his biological parents. On the road, he met a threatening old man, and slew him, not knowing that he was Laïus. Continuing on his way, he defeated the Sphinx. As a reward, he was elected King of Thebes and took as his wife Laïus' widow, Jocasta. Following an inquiry aimed at unmasking Laïus' killer, Oedipus discovered that he had fulfilled the prediction of the oracle because he was the son of Laïus and Jocasta, not of the sovereigns of Corinth, and that he had killed his father and married his mother. Jocasta committed suicide and Oedipus blinded himself as a punishment for the parricide and incest that he had committed.

In Sophocles' tragedy, Oedipus does not know that he is the child of Laïus and Jocasta. Similarly, in the Oedipus complex, the child is unaware of his incestuous and parricidal impulses towards his parents. For the myth, as for the complex, it is a way of introducing the unconscious.

The direct Oedipus complex

The stage of the Oedipus complex is not only one during which parricidal and incestuous impulses are exacerbated, but also the period of the phallic stage, which coincides with it. Indeed, for Freud, the outcome of this complex revolves solely around the possession of the penis and phallic omnipotence, the only means of determining the difference between the sexes around the age of three or four. Inspired by the myth, Freud began by describing a direct Oedipus complex in boys and girls, before introducing the notion of an inverted Oedipus complex, completing the direct form.

In the direct form of the Oedipus complex, the young boy's first object of affection is his mother, whom he wants to have all to himself. Around the age of three, under the pressure of omnipotent libidinal and aggressive impulses that are difficult to contain, the love that the boy feels for his mother leads him to enter into rivalry with his father, whom he therefore begins to hate. He then fears that his father will castrate him – depriving him of his penis – on account of the incestuous wishes that he harbours towards his mother and his hate for him. Under the impact of castration anxiety, the boy finally gives up his hopes of fulfilling his omnipotent incestuous wishes towards his mother and, overcoming his Oedipus complex, enters the period of latency. Nevertheless, in the analysis of Little Hans, Freud saw that it was not only castration anxiety that led him to abandon the Oedipus complex, but also the love that he felt for his father, which had become stronger than his hate towards him (see Chapter Nine).

As for the girl, Freud thought at first that her Oedipus complex was symmetrical with that of the boy: the girl's love for her father leads her to enter into rivalry with her mother, whom she begins to hate. However, as we have seen, because the girl only has knowledge of the male organ and is unaware of the existence of her female genitals, she feels intense penis envy. This penis envy strengthens the girl's hate for her mother, whom she reproaches for not having provided her with one. Disappointed, she turns away from her mother and towards her father in order to have a child with him. In this way the girl can overcome her Oedipus complex thanks to the symbolic equivalence "penis = child", the child making up for the penis that she does not have. This is what enables her, according to Freud, to give up her envy for the male organ.

Later on, Freud realised that the psychosexual development of girls differs fundamentally from that of boys. If, at the beginning of life, boys and girls take their mother as their love-object, their subsequent development diverges: the boy begins by being attached to his mother, and she is the one he wants to marry when the oedipal situation arises: on the other hand, if, at the beginning of life, the girl is also attached to her mother, she is led to change object when faced with the oedipal situation, that is, to give up her mother and to turn towards her father, who becomes the new object of her desire.

In *The Ego and the Id* (1923a), Freud was to draw on the notion of psychic bisexuality to affirm the existence of an inverted Oedipus complex alongside the direct Oedipus complex (see Chapter Twelve).

The decline of the Oedipus complex

The Oedipus complex "dissolves" or "disappears" in boys around the age of five. In fact, what disappears are the manifestations of the Oedipus complex at its height; for when the complex has been overcome, the oedipal situation proper disappears from consciousness and is included in infantile amnesia. Nevertheless, the oedipal situation subsists in the unconscious as a central organiser of the individual's psychic life, having lost its pathogenic character linked to the notion of "complex".

Defences against parricidal and incestuous impulses

From the psychoanalytic point of view, myths not only reflect the nature of unconscious interpersonal conflicts characteristic of human nature, but they also dramatise the defences aimed at rejecting outside of consciousness the impulses that are intolerable for it. In the case of the Oedipus complex, it is repression that fulfils this function. In the normal individual, once the period of latency has begun, only traces of parricidal and incestuous impulses subsist in consciousness, for example, in a resemblance that can be seen between the early object-choices, the father and the mother, and the object-choices made from the post-pubertal period onwards. In the neurotic, on the other hand, the psychic forces are not strong enough to maintain the repression and what we have is a *return of the repressed*, for example, the persistence of an excessive attachment to one of the parents and excessive hate for the other, or the appearance of psychic or somatic symptoms, anxieties, behavioural disorders and so on.

If repression is in the foreground, another equally important defence mechanism remains in the shadows: the division of Oedipus's parents into a couple that abandons and a couple that adopts (Quinodoz, 2002). Strangely enough, Laïus and Jocasta have only held the attention of the majority of psychoanalysts. And yet, if we take into account the presence of Polybus and Merope, respecting the myth, this division throws fresh light on an unconscious mode of functioning that is as universal as repression. In effect, it is a matter of an opposition between an idealised couple, that is, the couple of the adoptive parents, and a couple of dangerous parents, the biological parents – a characteristic opposition based on denial and splitting, both of which are more primitive defence mechanisms than repression. In psychoanalysis, when an individual considers that his/her mother (or his/her father) is either entirely good or entirely bad, he/she is unable to see that one and the same person is both good and bad, and that one can have murderous impulses towards a loved person. In the case of Oedipus, as his love for his biological parents did not temper his feelings of hate towards them, owing to the division, there was nothing to restrain his murderous and incestuous acts. It is only when the two parental couples reappear in consciousness that Oedipus realises that he has betrayed the love that he felt for Laïus and Jocasta and, overwhelmed by a sense of guilt, he blinds himself by way of punishment, alas, too late to work through his complex.

Chapter 8

The transference, the psychoanalytic setting and technique

The analysis of Dora and the discovery of the transference

Like the Oedipus complex, the notion of transference appeared gradually in Freud's work until it became a major motor of the psychoanalytic treatment. When he used the term transference for the first time in the *Studies on Hysteria* (1895), he considered it as a simple form of resistance without attributing more importance to it than that. It was in 1905, in connection with the treatment of Dora, that he recounted his discovery of the real nature of the transference.

Dora was twenty-one years old when she consulted Freud on the account of symptoms that she had been experiencing following a love affair between her father and Frau K., the wife of Herr K., a friend of her father's, at a time when both families were on holiday. Herr K., who was furious at being betrayed, started making advances to Dora, the daughter of his rival. One day, Herr K. suddenly took Dora in his arms and kissed her on the mouth. During her treatment, Dora admitted that she had felt sexual excitement through her contact with Herr K., due to the "pressure of his erect member against her body" (1905c, p. 30). After this incident, Dora left the holiday resort and began experiencing nervous symptoms and depression, and even threatened to commit suicide. The treatment lasted just eleven weeks. At that time, Freud's technique consisted essentially in reconstructing the chain of unconscious events that had led to the formation of the symptoms. He proceeded in this way with Dora and was much encouraged on verifying the soundness of his hypotheses concerning the sexual origin of hysterical symptoms and their resolution. For example, when Dora dreamt that she was fleeing from the scene of a house on fire, Freud saw this as confirmation of how dreams reveal unconscious conflicts, the fire representing symbolically for Dora the danger and pleasure of prohibited sexual excitement. Moreover, he noticed the value of his interpretations when Dora's cough disappeared after he had made a connection between this symptom and an eroticization of the buccal erogenous zone, reminding her of Herr K.'s kiss. Another dream revealed that Dora had the wish to replace Herr K. by her father. But Freud had not yet understood that Dora was transposing on to Herr K. the feelings she had for her father; he had not yet grasped the role played by the transference. Immersed in the search for Dora's memories and reconstruction, Freud did not see the underlying resistances that his explanations were arousing in his patient.

The lessons of a broken off treatment

It was with surprise that he saw Dora break off her sessions after only three months of treatment. On re-reading his notes, he became aware that it was not enough to communicate to his patient the reconstructed ideas, but that part of the treatment was played out at a deeper level, namely, that of unconscious affects relived in the here and now of the analytic relationship, without the patient or the analyst knowing it. After Dora's departure, Freud detected many warning signs of the impending interruption. For example, he recalled that Dora's dreams made mention of a smell of smoke (Herr K., Dora's father, and Freud were all three smokers), and it was only *later* that he linked these elements to the transference that had escaped him: "Taking into consideration, finally, the indications which seemed to point to there having been a transference on to me – since I am a smoker too – I came to the conclusion that the idea had probably occurred to her one day during a session that she would like to have a kiss from me" (1905c, p. 74). Thus the transference takes on the form of a repetition of emotions experienced in the past and then relived and transposed – transferred – on to the person of the psychoanalyst. In the case of Dora, the repetition consisted both in an unconscious wish to receive a kiss from Freud, in order to reproduce the prohibited sexual excitement already experienced with the man who seduced her, Herr K., and in the breaking off of the treatment, an unconscious reproduction of Dora's flight from Herr K., and her wish to take vengeance on her seducer, himself a representative of the father.

But Freud made use of this therapeutic failure when he realised retrospectively that a resistance linked to the transference had appeared without his realising it. Instead of leaving things there, he concluded that if he had identified this obstacle in time, he could have interpreted it and probably, thereby, have prevented his patient from breaking off the analysis. "Transference," he writes, "which seems ordained to be the greatest obstacle to psychoanalysis, becomes its most powerful ally, if its presence can be detected each time and explained to the patient" (p. 117).

The psychoanalytic setting

At the time of Dora's treatment, the conditions of the classical psychoanalytic treatment were not dissimilar to those we are familiar with today. The aim of the couch/armchair arrangement is to create the optimal conditions for the unfolding of the process. Thus Freud devoted one hour a day to each of his patients and saw them five or six times a week, except on rare occasions. He asked them to lie down on the couch, while he sat down behind them in order to better "isolate the transference", and also because he did not like being looked at. At the beginning of each treatment, he would begin by asking the patient to follow faithfully the "fundamental rule of psychoanalysis", that is, to say everything that came into his/her mind, while "suspending the temptation to judge and select". At the same time, he recommended that the analyst should adopt an attitude of "evenly-suspended attention" and avoid taking notes during the session so as not to disturb the process of listening. He noted that he saw little value in "the keeping of a shorthand record" (1912, p. 113);

for according to him, the exactness of written analytic observations is necessarily only apparent, and cannot be a substitute "for actual presence at an analysis" (p. 114). Freud considered that psychoanalysis was first and foremost designed to treat neuroses, an affection in which the therapist's personality plays a decisive role. With experience, he gradually moved away from an "active" technique, in which he had the tendency to impose his own reconstructions on his patient, preferring a technique based on trust in the patient. From this perspective, he advised analysts to let themselves be surprised, to retain a detached attitude, and to avoid preconceived ideas.

In 1910, during the period when Freud was writing his recommendations on technique, he founded the International Psychoanalytic Association so that the psychoanalytic method he had created could develop under better conditions while retaining its specificity.

New developments to the concept of transference

Freud never wrote a work entirely devoted to psychoanalytic technique. On the other hand, he published various short texts in which he related his experience as a practitioner in a familiar tone, in the form of recommendations. Among these, it is worth noting the developments he contributed to the notion of transference.

Freud states that the phenomenon of transference is not exclusive to psychoanalysis. He distinguishes between the *transferences* that are a feature of everyday life, in particular in loving relationships, and the *transference* proper, which he considers as an artificial illness that can be resolved by psychoanalysis. This artificial illness – or *transference neurosis* – is characterised on the one hand by the displacement of an internalised relationship with a person of the past on to the person of the psychoanalyst in the present and, on the other, by the compulsive repetition of a traumatic situation at the origin of the patient's suffering. Freud gives a nice example of displacement on to his person during the analysis of the "Rat Man" (see below, Chapter Nine). The patient tells him in the first session that his obsessions began in the army, the day when he heard a captain describing with delight a Chinese torture in which rats bored their way into the anus of a victim. After listening to his patient's account, Freud began to explain in detail that his symptoms had a sexual origin. He was then surprised to have confirmation of his patient's transference on to him when the latter unwittingly addressed Freud on several occasions as "My captain" (1909b, p. 169).

Repeating instead of remembering

A certain number of patients do not recall their past and cannot communicate their experiences which date back to a time before the emergence of verbal language. That is why they are condemned to *repeat* instead of *remembering*. Freud shows that memories that have apparently been forgotten by these patients may reappear in the form of behavioural symptoms in everyday life and are reproduced in the transference relationship with the psychoanalyst (Freud, 1914). For example, it may be the case that a patient who experienced a situation of abandonment in early childhood cannot remember it, is incapable of speaking about it, and that, having become an adult, cannot prevent him from re-enacting this abandonment. He may, for example, regularly break off relations with those with whom he had wanted to establish lasting contact, whether in friendship or in professional life. In the course of analysis, this patient will tend to reproduce this situation of abandonment, for instance, by threatening to break off his treatment prematurely on various pretexts. It follows from this that the psychoanalyst will have to treat the illness not as an event of the past – which the patient cannot remember –, but "as a present-day force" (p. 151). When the patient succeeds in becoming aware that he is *doing* something in the transference relationship which reproduces a situation already lived through in the past, and he is able to recall the conditions under which this traumatic situation appeared, the displacement ceases and the repetition is no longer reproduced: the transference is thus resolved.

Love and hate in the transference and counter-transference

Freud also takes into account the affective components of love and hate that the patient feels in the transference in relation to the psychoanalyst. He distinguishes between a *positive* transference, dominated by tender feelings, and a *negative* transference, dominated by hostile feelings. When the positive transference is too intense, as in the case of an excessive transference-love, it may be the sign of resistance: Freud advises the analyst who is struggling with such a situation not to break off the treatment, for this transference would simply be repeated, unchanged, with other therapists. Nor must one mistake this love for a manifestation of real love towards the person of the psychoanalyst, but rather take it as the expression of the transference and it must be analysed as such. To illustrate the role played by the transference when it is not recognised by the analyst, Freud gives the example of the end of the treatment of Anna O. with Joseph Breuer (see above, Chapter Two). According to Freud, Breuer broke off the treatment of this patient because he had been frightened by the sexual nature of her loving feelings towards him, and because he thought that this relationship was a danger for his marriage. In other words, if Breuer had known that what was involved was a transference, he might have understood that Anna O. was displacing on to the person of her therapist the love that she felt for her father. Instead of that, Breuer reacted by believing that his patient's feelings were directed solely at his person and were a real threat to his marital relationship.

Freud rarely mentions the notion of *countertransference*. He saw it solely as a reaction of opposition on the part of the analyst who had not sufficiently elaborated the patient's transference. Thereafter, the notion of the countertransference continued to evolve and post-Freudian psychoanalysts would regard it as a major instrument for elaborating the transference within the psychoanalytic relationship.

Chapter 9

Four of Freud's clinical observations

Little Hans: the first psychoanalysis of a child (Freud, 1909a)

Aged five, Little Hans – his real name was Herbert Graf – had been suffering recently from a phobia that led him to refuse to go out of the house and into the street for fear of being bitten by a horse. His analysis was carried out by his father, the composer and musical critic Max Graf, and supervised by Freud who was to publish his notes with the father's permission. In 1922, Freud received a visit from Hans, who was now a young man in good health: he had no recollections of his treatment. He became a renowned opera producer, notably at the Metropolitan Opera in New York. He died in Geneva in 1973. Both the father's observations and those of Freud supported the hypotheses formulated in the *Three Essays on the Theory of Sexuality* (1905b).

The early role of sexuality in the child is confirmed

The faithful transcription of this young man's statements shows that his mind was constantly preoccupied by the enigma of sexuality. Like all children of his age, Little Hans was relentlessly curious and interested in his own penis – his "widdler", as he called it, – and wanted to know if his mother also had a widdler. One day, when he was about

3½ years old, his mother was getting undressed: "What are you staring like that for?" she asked. Hans: "I was only looking to see if you'd got a widdler too." His mother: "Of course. Didn't you know that?" Hans: "No. I thought you were so big you'd have a widdler like a horse" (pp. 9–10). What Little Hans said here confirmed for Freud the theory that the child only has knowledge of one genital organ, the male organ, so that the possession of (or lack of) the penis acquired a decisive role in the psychosexual development of both boys and girls.

Castration anxiety

This anxiety reaches its peak around the age of three or four, as on the day when Hans's mother found him with his hand on his penis: "If you do that, I shall send for Dr. A. to cut off your widdler. And then what'll you widdle with?" she asked. Hans: "With my bottom" (pp. 7–8). As for the girl, "deprived of the penis", her so-called "castration" gives rise in the boy to a denial of this lack and leads him to attribute to the girl a penis that she does not have. Nevertheless, in this text, Freud evokes the idea that Little Hans might have envisaged the existence of a vagina: "If matters had lain entirely in my hands, I should have ventured to give the child the one remaining piece of enlightenment which his parents withheld from him. I should have confirmed his instinctive premonitions, by telling him of the existence of the vagina and of copulation; thus I should have still further diminished his unresolved residue, and put an end to the stream of questions" (p. 145). His remark on the early perception of the existence of the vagina was an isolated instance, and he did not link it up with his conception of female sexuality.

The general value of the oedipal conflict in the child

Hans' wish to sleep with his mother and to receive "coaxes" from her appeared during the summer holidays, when his father was absent. The little boy had expressed the wish that his father should "go away" and "stay away", and even formulated a wish that he should be "dead".

For Freud this death wish towards his father can be found in every little boy and is part of the normal Oedipal situation; but when it is exacerbated, this wish can become the source of symptoms, as was the case with Little Hans. It is in this way that the conflict of ambivalence between love and hate becomes a central issue in the oedipal situation: "But this father, whom he could not help hating as a rival, was the same father whom he had always loved and was bound to go on loving, who had been his model, had been his first playmate, and had looked after him from his earliest infancy: and this was what gave rise to the first conflict. Nor could this conflict find an immediate solution" (p. 134).

The cure of an infantile phobia

The real cause of the phobia lay in the death wishes that Hans harboured towards his father, for these were repressed in the unconscious. Having such feelings of hatred towards a loved father became unacceptable for the child's conscious mind, which is why these aggressive impulses were repressed, and the fear of being castrated by the father was displaced in the form of being bitten or knocked over by a horse. Having arrived at this crucial point, the treatment came to a standstill. So Freud decided to intervene. Seeing the boy and his father together, he understood that details in the appearance of the horses that frightened little Hans probably reminded him of his father's glasses and moustache. He communicated this discovery to the little boy. This interpretation of the little boy's transference on to his father opened up the path of recovery; for the explanation given by Freud enabled the child to become aware of the reasons why he had displaced on to the animal both his death wishes towards his father and his fear of being castrated by him.

The Rat Man: treatment of an obsessional neurosis (Freud, 1909b)

Ernst Lanzer − known as the "Rat Man" − was a jurist, aged 29, when he consulted Freud in 1907 on account of multiple obsessions and inhibitions which were a handicap for him in his professional and emotional life. The treatment lasted nine months, from October 1907 to July 1908. When he had recovered, the patient found work again but, after being mobilized in 1914, he died shortly after the beginning of the First World War.

Obsessional disorders have a psychic origin

His illness was characterised by striking compulsive disorders resulting in severe limitations such as ruminations, various rituals, and compulsions to perform undesirable acts. For a long time it was thought that such symptoms were the result of a degeneration or organic weakness of the mind. From the very first session, Freud received confirmation that the obsessional symptoms of his patient could be resolved by psychoanalysis. Indeed, the free associations produced by Ernst Lanzer allowed Freud to establish a link between a frightening voyeuristic obsession (seeing women naked) and the recollection that this obsession had begun around the age of six or seven, at a time when a young governess took him into her bed and let him caress her. These early sexual experiences, accompanied by great excitation and intolerable guilt feelings, had created in the mind of the young boy an insoluble psychic conflict, characteristic of a neurosis, and thus curable by psychoanalysis.

Resolution of the great obsessive fear of rats

It was the analysis of the great obsessive fear of rats that enabled Freud to go further in the investigation of the real causes of this obsessional neurosis and the possibilities of clearing up the symptoms. Everything had begun recently in the month of August 1907, when the patient was in the army and had heard a captain reciting the details of a horrible oriental torture: a pot, with rats in it, was turned upside down on a criminal's bottom so that they bored their way into his anus. Since hearing this story, the patient had been terrified by the obsessive idea that this punishment would be carried out on his father, and then on his "lady". So, in order to fend off this intolerable thought, he repeated a gesture of repudiation accompanied by the incantatory phrase: "Whatever are you thinking of?" Freud also noted that at each important moment of the story, the patient's face took on a very strange expression that seemed to translate his "horror at pleasure of his own of which he was unaware" (1909b, p. 167). This story was the point of departure for a detailed analysis of multiple obsessional thoughts and acts from which the patient suffered, using systematically the method of free association. At the end of this work of painstaking unravelling, Freud succeeded in clearing up one idea after another and each compulsive act of his patient.

The ruthless struggle between love and hate

The real significance of such acts lies in the fact that the obsessional symptom juxtaposes two contradictory tendencies, love and hate, in such a way that these antithetical tendencies are carried out simultaneously. But the component of hate escapes the patient's conscious mind which justifies his act by means of rationalisation, that is, by scarcely credible justifications that are aimed at masking the hate so that it remains repressed in the unconscious: "The love has not succeeded in extinguishing the hatred but only driving it down into the unconscious; and, in the unconscious the hatred, safe from the danger of being destroyed by the operations of consciousness, is able to persist and even to grow" (1909b, p. 239).

Anal eroticism

The theme of anal eroticism is omnipresent in this treatment, but Freud does not go into it more deeply in connection with the Rat Man. He subsequently devoted several articles to obsessional neurosis, noting in particular the symbolic links that may be observed between money and anal eroticism, which determines the particular character traits of obsessional neurotics: for example, the compulsive need for cleanliness linked to the obsessive fear of contamination; the equivalence between money and excrement; the equivalence between rats and children; or again, the infantile sexual belief that children are born through the anus.

Neurotic and psychotic elements side by side

Freud speaks of "neurosis" in connection with the diagnosis of the Rat Man, but on many occasions he notes elements that belong more to psychosis than neurosis. For example, he uses the term "delirium" (p. 164), when describing the patient's compulsion to interrupt his work at night and to open the door in expectation of his father's arrival, even though he knew that he had died nine years before. This type of belief constitutes a disavowal of reality that is characteristic of psychotic thought. But it was only at the end of the 1930s that Freud would recognise the coexistence of psychotic and neurotic elements not only in psychosis, but also in neurosis and in the normal individual.

President Schreber's autobiography: a case of paranoia (Freud, 1911)

Having devoted himself to discovering the origin of the neuroses, Freud set out to discover a specific mechanism of psychosis. He found the clinical material he was seeking not in one of his patients, but in *Memoirs of my Nervous Illness* by Daniel Paul Schreber (1903), a German jurist whom Freud never met. Schreber was forty-two years old in 1884 when he was hospitalised for the first time for depression. Ten years later, when he was President of the Appeal Court in Saxony, Schreber developed a syndrome of acute hallucinatory delirium. He was hospitalised in Dresden for eight years before pleading his own cause before a tribunal and obtaining his release. It was in the context of these proceedings that he described his illness in detail, his delirium and his hallucinations, bringing together a body of particularly rich clinical material. He died in 1911 in a psychiatric asylum in Leipzig, the year Freud published his study. It is also worth noting that Daniel Paul was the son of Gottlieb Moritz Schreber, a doctor who had become well known for his particularly severe, indeed sadistic principles of physical education.

The fear of being transformed into a woman

In its acute phase, Schreber's paranoiac and hallucinatory delirium consisted essentially of very frightening delusions of persecution, centred on the idea that he had to be emasculated and transformed into a woman, and that he could not escape this sexual abuse. His persecutor was first the famous Professor Flechsig, his referring physician, and then God himself. Schreber obtained confirmation of this persecution through voices that spoke to him and through experiences of the destruction of various organs, such as his stomach or his intestines. Later, these persecutory delusions with a sexual basis turned into delusions of redemption. Thus the obsessive idea of being transformed into a woman had become a mystical project, one of being fecundated by the divine rays in order to engender new human beings. This mission associated him with God, towards whom he felt a mixture of veneration and revolt, especially because he demanded from Schreber, a man of high morality, voluptuous sexual pleasure similar to that which, in his imagination, only a woman can feel.

Delusion: an attempted cure

But why had Flechsig, who had cured Schreber of his first illness, now become a persecutor? For Freud, it is precisely the person who has first been loved and admired, and to whom great influence has been attributed, who becomes the persecutor, love turning into hate. Why such a reversal? Because Schreber's sense of recognition towards Flechsig was based on an intense erotic attachment towards this doctor: it was a "transference process", Freud notes. It was this attachment that led Schreber to want to become the wife of such a marvellous human being as Flechsig. During a later transformation of the delirium, the persecutor Flechsig was in turn replaced by God so that the homosexual fantasy became more acceptable to Schreber, for emasculation and transformation into a woman became part of a divine plan thanks to a process of "rationalisation". This transformation of the delusion led Freud to say "the delusional formation, which we take to be the pathological product, is in reality an attempt at recovery, a process of reconstruction" (1911, p. 71).

Schreber's paranoia: a paternal complex

Freud concluded that Schreber's conflict with Flechsig, and then with God, proved, in the light of analysis, to be based on an infantile conflict with his much-loved father, so that what determined the delirium was a mechanism similar to the mechanism that produces a neurosis. Freud postulated that Schreber's father had appeared in his son's eyes as a severe and imposing figure, forbidding the boy from enjoying auto-erotic sexual satisfaction and threatening to punish it with castration. In other words, the wish to be transformed into a woman – which forms the nucleus of Daniel Paul's delusional formation – was nothing other than the fear of being castrated by his father because of infantile mas-turbation, which led the son to adopt a passive homosexual position, or "feminine position of the boy", characteristic of the ambivalence in the paternal complex consisting of a mixture of submission and revolt.

The narcissistic stage of infantile development

Following up these reflections, Freud puts forward the hypothesis that the homosexual tendencies can be found at a *stage* of infantile sexual evolution called the *narcissistic stage* of development, an intermedi-ate stage between auto-erotism and object-love. Consequently, when the moment of heterosexual object-choice is reached during normal development, the homosexual tendencies do not disappear completely. They *underpin* the foundations of friendship and camaraderie towards persons of the same sex.

However, in pathological cases, the narcissistic stage of infan-tile development may function as a "point of fixation" or a "point of regression" and establish itself as a "weak point" of the personality, which lends itself to paranoia, that is, persecutory anxieties. Freud was to return to these questions when he developed the notion of "psychic bisexuality" in 1923 (see Chapter Twelve).

The analysis of an infantile neurosis: the Wolf Man (Freud, 1918 [1914])

Sergueï Constantinovitch Pankejeff, a young and wealthy Russian aris-tocrat, aged 23 – pseudonym the "Wolf Man" – came to see Freud in 1910 on account of severe psychic disorders considered to be incurable by the most eminent European psychiatrists he had consulted hitherto.

Everything had begun with a depression at the age of eighteen, following the suicide of his father and his sister. He had become incapacitated to the point that he could no longer go anywhere alone without being accompanied by his valet and his personal physician. The analysis lasted four years and ended in 1914 after the term had been fixed in advance by Freud himself, who then claimed he had been completely cured. He immediately wrote up an account of the case, focusing solely on the analysis of the infantile neurosis. Sergueï returned to Odessa and, after being ruined by the revolution of October 1917, returned to Vienna. In 1920, Freud saw him again for a brief analysis, then, in 1926, entrusted him to Ruth Mack Brunswick, who succeeded in analysing his delusions of persecution. Increasingly identified with the Wolf Man, Sergueï was supported financially by the psychoanalytic community and by the psychoanalyst Muriel Gardiner, with whose help he succeeded in writing his *Memoirs* in 1971. He died in Vienna in 1979.

An infantile neurosis in various stages

Sergueï's neurosis had undergone several successive transformations before it reappeared when he was eighteen. Freud learned that at around the age of three, Sergueï's character had changed dramatically and that, from being a sweet and peaceful child he suddenly became irritable, violent and sadistic. A second change occurred around the age of five, when anxieties and phobias appeared, in particular the fear of being devoured by a wolf; a third change, after the phobias had been replaced by obsessional symptoms with a religious content, involved praying and insulting God alternately. Around the age of eight, his symptoms disappeared and the child led a normal life until the age of eighteen.

A stream of early seductions

During the analysis, Sergueï's first memories allowed Freud to attribute the first change of character to a series of seductions involving successively the English governess, Sergueï's sister, and his nurse Nanya. These events triggered in the little boy castration anxieties capable of explaining his change of character. At the same time, these seductions led, according to Freud, to a regression to the sadistic-anal stage, with the result that Serguei had adopted a "passive feminine position" towards women, and then towards his father, seeking in particular to be punished by him.

The dream about the wolves

The patient reported a dream that enabled Freud to account for the second change that occurred around the age of five, at a time when Serguei was beginning to present anxieties and phobias. In this frightening dream, the patient was lying in his bed when the window suddenly swung open. He saw six or seven wolves with long tails, sitting on a walnut tree and looking at him with their ears pricked. Serguei woke up in terror of being eaten by the wolves.

Freud took as his starting-point a series of associations by his patient: "A real occurrence – dating from a very early period – looking – immobility – sexual problems – castration – his father – something terrible" (1918 [1914], p. 34). He made a series of deductions that led him to believe that the child had probably witnessed his parents having sexual intercourse at an even earlier age of one and a half. But why was there so much anxiety? Various elements led Freud to think that the little boy had seen himself in his mother's place as a victim of his father and that the sight of this scene had triggered castration anxieties that were displaced from the image of his father on to the wolves.

A real or imaginary scene?

Could such a primal scene really have been witnessed by such a young child or was it imagined in a retroactive phantasy? Freud is of the opinion that if the analysis goes deep enough, the analyst will in the end be persuaded that the perception of such a scene at the age of one and a half is entirely possible. However, at this very tender age, the child does not yet have sufficient means to understand what is happening, and can only elaborate his first impressions by means of a "deferred revision" (p. 48), once his psychosexual development has evolved. From the technical point of view, Freud adds that during the course of the treatment the analyst can provisionally consider such phantasies as real and that "the difference [will] only come at the end of the analysis, after the phantasies [have] been laid bare" (p. 50). In other words, it is a matter of waiting until the patient has acquired sufficient capacity to distinguish phantasy from reality.

From phobia to obsessional neurosis

For Freud, the transformation of the phobic symptoms into obsessional symptoms towards the age of four no doubt resulted from a displacement of Sergu 00ef's masochistic attitude towards his father on to the image of the relationship of Christ to God the Father. Freud thinks that the influence of the religious education given to him by his mother, as well as by his private tutor, had a role to play in this.

Anal eroticism

Freud pursues his hypotheses by showing that there are close relations between money and anal erotism. For example, he establishes a connection between the paradoxical behaviour of this wealthy patient who was sometimes miserly and sometimes lavish, and an alternation between constipation and constant enemas. The disorders of bowel functioning not only marked his character, which was dominated by doubt, but also the way in which the little boy formed a troubling image of adult sexuality as well as of his own. In other words, the child had acquired a conception of the primal scene that was essentially based on a "cloacal theory" (p. 79), for want of having developed sufficient knowledge of the difference between the sexes and of the role of genital sexuality in women. The idea that a woman could be castrated reinforced the little boy's castration anxiety in relation to his own penis, which increased his identification with women, as well as his feminine passive position towards men. Freud goes a step further and establishes the following equivalence: "faeces" = gift = baby".

A termination fixed in advance

This case observation was the account of the longest psychoanalytic treatment conducted by Freud. The analysis ended on a note of success that calls for two technical remarks. On the one hand Freud justifies the length of the analysis by noting that the duration of a psychoanalytic treatment is necessarily proportionate to the gravity of the symptoms; on the other, he explains that he was led to use an unusual technical procedure in order to overcome the patient's resistances. He fixed the end of this analysis one year in advance and was surprised that the approaching end had the effect of removing the ultimate obstacles to its successful completion.

Chapter 10

Metapsychology (1915–1917)

A point of arrival and a point of departure

A term invented by Freud, derived from the Greek prefix *meta* ("after" or "beyond"), "metapsychology" is to the observation of psychological facts what metaphysics is to the observation of the facts of the physical world. Freud thus passes over from a descriptive clinical level to a level of theoretical abstraction, and proposes models of the functioning of the human mind of general significance. Take for example the notion of "drive". Freud introduces this term to describe the pressure that leads the human being to nourish himself and procreate. He names the first "self-preservative drives" and the second "sexual drives". As the "drive" is an abstract notion, we never encounter a drive as such, but we perceive it indirectly through the effects that it produces or through what represents it. Thus the sexual drive can either manifest itself in a variety of ways through the emotions arising from an erotic desire towards a person, through the words expressing this desire, or it can appear in the scenario of a dream. The *Papers on Metapsychology* constitute a series of texts that are often arduous for readers who are not very familiar with clinical experience but, in Freud's mind, the link between theory and clinical practice is constantly present.

The *Papers on Metapsychology* are at once a point of arrival and a point of departure from the point of view of the evolution of Freudian thought. First they represent the culmination of over thirty years of clinical experience which led Freud to propose a synthetic model of normal and pathological mental functioning. Known under the name of the "first Freudian topography", it was founded on the distinction between unconscious, preconscious and conscious, and of the "first drive theory", founded on the principle of pleasure/unpleasure. At the same time the work opens up new perspectives which give greater account to object-relations, identifications, the effects of love and hate and the unconscious sense of guilt. The ideas presented in the *Papers on Metapsychology* would serve as a basis for the notions of ego, id and superego which Freud was to introduce in 1923 (see Chapter Twelve). Far from contradicting themselves, these different points of view add complementary perspectives, just as one may describe a construction from different angles, according to its forms, dimensions, and spaces.

Freud had planned to publish all the twelve essays that make up the *Papers on Metapsychology*. In reality he only published five of them: "Instincts and their vicissitudes" (1915a), "Repression" (1915b), "The unconscious" (1915c), 'A Metapsychological supplement to the theory of dreams' (1917a) and "Mourning and melancholia" (1917b); the sixth, "A Phylogenetic Fantasy – Overview of the Transference Neuroses" was found again in 1983 (Freud, 1987). In order to present these rich and complex texts, I will only dwell on the papers "Instincts and their vicissitudes" and "Mourning and melancholia". This limited choice, rather than a condensed study of them all, will enable me to demonstrate the theoretical and clinical approach that Freud adopted in this work.

"Instincts and their vicissitudes" (1915a)

What is a drive?

Freud defines the drive (in German *Trieb, S.E.* "instinct") as a pressure with a source, an aim, and an object. The drive has its *source* in the organism in the form of a need – for nourishment or of a sexual nature – which can only be suppressed through its satisfaction, which, according to Freud, is the *aim* of every drive. As for the *object* of the drive – the means by which it can reach its aim – it can be an external object, such as a person, or a part of one's own body. The task of mastering drive excitations is the task of the nervous system and, when they reach it, to reduce them to the lowest level possible. The drives are automatically modulated by the sensations of pleasure and unpleasure, a principle that Freud calls the *pleasure/unpleasure principle.* At this stage of the evolution of his thought, he considered that this principle applied to every drive whose ultimate aim was no other than that of seeking pleasure and of avoiding unpleasure.

There are many sorts of drives, but Freud reduces them to two fundamental groups: the group of the *ego-drives* or *drives of self-preservation* – for which the model is hunger and the feeding function – and the group of the *sexual drives.* In the course of development, the sexual drives are underpinned by the drives of self-preservation which supply them with a source of organic energy, a direction, and an object; it is only when the child abandons the hope of fulfilling his incestuous wishes towards his real and fantasised external objects that the sexual drives free themselves from the drives of self-preservation and become autonomous. In the light of his experience acquired in the treatment of the neuroses, Freud examined the various *vicissitudes* of the drives, that is, the various modes of defence that are set up against the drives in order to oppose their activity. The first vicissitude concerns the aim of the drive, which may transform itself into its contrary; the second vicissitude concerns the object which may be an independent person or the subject's own person. For example, if one considers the turning round of sadism into masochism, it can be seen that masochism implies an inversion of roles between the one who inflicts and the one who is subjected to the suffering. Freud also examines the analogous transformations between voyeurism and exhibitionism.

Love and hate at the beginning of life

Freud devotes a significant part of "Instincts and their vicissitudes" to the question of love and hate, and thus to ambivalence. With the benefit of experience, he was able to see that these complex affects played a decisive role in the intrapsychic conflicts of his patients. A series of different lines of questioning led Freud to write some particularly inspired pages.

Originally, the ego is cathected by the drives, which it partly satisfies itself: this is the primordial narcissistic state in which the ego has no need of the outer world because it is auto-erotic. Thereafter, when the ego cannot avoid feeling unpleasant internal excitations – such as hunger and the need to be nourished by external intervention – it is obliged to emerge from its auto-erotic state and venture to meet objects. The impact that these objects in the external world have on the ego brings about a fundamental reorganisation in relation to the polarity pleasure-unpleasure: "in so far as the objects which are presented to [the ego] are sources of pleasure, it takes them into itself, 'introjects' them (to use Ferenczi's term); and, on the other hand, it expels whatever within itself becomes a cause of unpleasure" (1915a, p. 136). A primordial division of the ego is effected, which is no longer a simple division between inside (ego-subject) and outside (indifferent and unpleasant), but between a "pleasure-ego" which includes objects that are a source of satisfaction and an *external world* that becomes a source of unpleasure because it is perceived as alien and extraneous. The intervention of the object at the stage of primary narcissism thus sets up the opposition between "hating" and "loving".

Love, expression of the total sexual tendency

Consequently, when the object is a source of pleasure, we say that we "love" the object; and, when it is a source of unpleasure, we "hate" it. But, Freud asks himself, can we say of a drive, in everyday language, that it "loves" the object? Of course not, he replies, no more than we can say of a drive that it "hates" the object. That is why, he insists, "the attitudes of love and hate cannot be made use of for the relations of *instincts* to their objects, but are reserved for the relations of the *total ego* to objects" (p. 137, Freud's emphasis). What is the status, then, of the word *love* when it is fully accomplished? Freud considers unequivocally that love appears at the genital stage after there has been a synthesis of the component drives within a *total ego*: ". . . the relation of the ego to its sexual object [is] the most appropriate case in which to employ the word 'love' – this fact teaches us that the word can only begin to be applied in this relation after there has been a synthesis of all the component instincts of sexuality under the primacy of the genitals and in the service of the reproductive function" (pp. 137–138).

As for the origin of hate, according to Freud it is to be found less in sexual life than in the ego's struggle for self-preservation, that is, in the hate felt towards the object which does not satisfy the drives of self-preservation. It is at the level of self-preservation that the origin of the conflict of ambivalence is to be found, which is particularly evident in the neuroses.

Freud then goes on to describe the preliminary stages of love, beginning with the first aim, the phase of *incorporating* or *devouring*, an ambivalent stage par excellence in which the individual does not know if he destroys the object through love or through hate; this stage is followed by the sadistic-anal pregenital stage and, finally, by the genital stage: "not until the genital organisation is established does love become the opposite of hate" (p. 139). He notes that hate is older than love; subsequently, love appears when the ego becomes a total ego. He concludes by mentioning the possibility that hate takes on an erotic character when it regresses to the sadistic stage, thereby heralding future developments concerning sadomasochism as well as the fundamental conflict between the life drive and the death drive (see Chapter Eleven).

"Mourning and melancholia" (1917b)

Distinguishing between normal mourning and pathological mourning

Following the studies by Karl Abraham on the psychoanalytic treatment of manic-depressive patients – at that time, what is known as depression today was called "melancholia" – Freud examined the differences between normal and pathological mourning. He noted that pathological mourning develops at an unconscious level and that the patient's aversion towards his own ego predominates in the form of self-reproaches and self-denigration. How are these self-accusations, which can even culminate in a delusional expectation of punishment, be explained? Freud had a brilliant intuition: he realised that the self-accusations of a depressive person are in fact accusations directed against a significant person, generally someone to whom he is closely related. Thus he says: "The woman who loudly pities her husband for being tied to such an incapable wife as herself is really accusing her *husband* of being incapable, in whatever sense she may mean this" (1917b, p. 248, Freud's emphasis). In other words, when this woman accuses herself by saying: "I am incapable!" this self-accusation turns out to be an accusation that is unconsciously directed at her husband: "*You* are incapable!" Following up on his intuition, Freud notes that the words used by the melancholic patient to formulate his or her self-accusations reveal point by point the structure of his or her internal conflict. He then breaks this down into its different elements.

"I am incapable!" means in fact: "You are incapable!"

Freud begins by showing that what underlies the substitution of the "*You*" for the "*I*" contained in the self-accusation: "*I* am incapable!" which is an implicit accusation of another person: "*You* are incapable!" Freud explains himself by showing that in the case of an object-loss there is a fundamental difference between normal mourning and pathological mourning, a difference that results in a change in direction of the object-cathexis. In normal mourning, the subject is capable of giving up the "lost" object – a real person or an ideal – and of withdrawing his libido from it, so that the free libido can be displaced on to a new object. In melancholia, however, the subject does not withdraw his cathexis from the lost object; his ego "swallows" this object in fantasy in order to unite with it rather than separating from it, thereby taking the path of *narcissistic identification.* It is this change of direction of the object-cathexis towards the ego itself, identified with the object, which explains the melancholic's lack of interest in the people about him and the resulting "narcissistic" withdrawal into himself; the patient is so preoccupied with himself that he is literally sucked into the whirlwind of his self-reproaches.

This turning round of the reproaches on to the subject's own person implies a splitting of the ego in which one part of the ego is identified with the lost object, while the other part criticises the first, adopting the position of a moral conscience, an agency Freud was subsequently to call the superego (see Chapter Twelve): "We see how in him one part of the ego sets itself over against the other, judges it critically, and, as it were, takes it as its object" (p. 247).

Love regresses to narcissistic identification and hate is turned round against the subject himself

The depressive patient's powerful tendency towards self-destruction, Freud continues, results from a strengthening of the ambivalence of love and hate towards the object and the ego, affects that are dissociated and undergo different vicissitudes. On the one hand the subject continues to love the object, but at the price of a return to a primitive form of love which is so-called "primary" or "narcissistic" identification. Here the libido regresses to the cannibalistic oral phase in which the subject wants to incorporate the object by "devouring" it. On the other hand, following the ego's narcissistic identification with the loved object, the subject's hate which was destined for the object in the external world turns round against his own ego, which is at one with the object: "If the love for the object – a love which cannot be given up though the object itself is given up – takes refuge in narcissistic identification, then the hate comes into operation on this substitutive object, abusing it, debasing it, making it suffer, and deriving sadistic satisfaction from its suffering" (p. 251).

Manifest self-reproaches: latent reproaches directed at others

Freud notes another decisive point by showing that the self-accusations of the melancholic are simultaneously an attack on the object, which means that the patient's apparent narcissistic withdrawal does not excluded the possibility that an unconscious object-relation persists. In fact, he observes that the melancholic patient, like the obsessional, derives *enjoyment* from exercising simultaneously unconscious trends of sadism and hate towards himself and towards others, the latter generally being someone in their immediate family circle: "In both disorders the patients usually still succeed, by the circuitous path of self-punishment, in taking revenge on the original object and in tormenting their loved one through their illness, having resorted to it in order to avoid the need to express their hostility to him openly" (p. 251). This narcissistic withdrawal no doubt led Freud to think that patients of this type – suffering from "narcissistic neuroses" – are incapable of establishing a transference, which makes them inaccessible to analysis. Later on, post-Freudian psychoanalysts would show that these patients do in fact establish a transference, and that a transference in which hostility towards the analyst predominates is analysable.

Chapter 11

The fundamental conflict between the life drive and the death drive

The pleasure of suffering

Freud started out with the idea that patients who suffer from neuroses seek the help of a psychoanalyst with the aim of being released from their symptoms and of rediscovering the pleasure of living. Their psychic functioning thus conforms to the pleasure/unpleasure principle which Freud presented as having general significance. But before too long this principle was contradicted by events in clinical practice: how does one explain that some patients cannot tolerate being relieved of their symptoms and fall ill again just at the moment when they should be getting better? Why do others reproduce traumatic experiences compulsively, with their countless forms of suffering? Where does the destructivity, which is sometimes taken to extremes, of depressive patients, drug addicts, perverse and psychotic patients come from?

From 1915 onwards, several publications by Freud reflect new concerns. Having described the bitter struggle between two parts of the ego that unfolds in the inner world of the depressive, and which can drive the individual to suicide ("Mourning and melancholia", 1917b), he brought together a number of case observations concerning patients suffering from the sadomasochistic fantasy of being beaten ("A child is being beaten", 1919). He notes that, in the obsession with being beaten, generally on the buttocks, the pleasure derived from the pain is intimately linked to the eroticization of the incestuous oedipal objects.

In a girl, this fantasy constitutes a regressive substitute for the unconscious incestuous wish towards the father, whereas in a man it is the
expression of a "passive feminine position", equally towards the father
and characteristic of male masochism. In "The psychogenesis of a case
of homosexuality in a woman" (1920a), Freud was led to break off
the treatment of his patient on account of an insurmountable hostile
transference which ultimately proved to be the repetition of a wish to
take vengeance on her father. Later on he was to name this paradoxical attitude a "negative therapeutic reaction". To ensure the success of
a treatment, Freud notes, it is indispensable that the analyst is able to
draw on solid motivation in the patient, on a positive transference, and
on sufficiently strong heterosexual tendencies.

Confrontation between death drive and life drive

In 1920, Freud wrote *Beyond the Pleasure Principle* (1920b), a
visionary and controversial work that marked a turning-point in his
evolution. He put forward a new hypothesis according to which an
individual's psychic functioning is governed by a more elementary
conflict than the pleasure/unpleasure principle, namely, the fundamental conflict between a life drive and a death drive. True enough, the
pleasure/unpleasure principle retains its full value but, for pleasure to
prevail over the tendency to unpleasure, the life drive must master the
death drive, at least in part. In other words, when the death drive predominates at the heart of this conflict, the destructive component of
psychic life imposes itself, as in sadism and masochism; on the other
hand, when the life drive predominates, the destructive component is
in part neutralised and aggressiveness is put in the service of life and
the ego. Freud initially presented this hypothesis as pure speculation,
but he was soon to accord it increasing importance.

Repetition, the compulsion to repeat and transference

In psychoanalysis, the simple fact of *repetition* is one of the means
used by the mind to master situations that generate anxiety and to avoid

them taking on a traumatic character. Thus repetition is part of normal infantile development and constitutes one of the means used by the young child to overcome his separation-anxieties. Freud illustrates this with reference to his grandson who, when he was aged one and a half would play untiringly at throwing away and reeling in a wooden reel on a string, while exclaiming *"Fort-Da"– disappearance/return –* with the aim of mastering his anxieties linked to the appearances/disappearances of his mother. Likewise, in traumatic neurosis, the repetition is an attempt to master a painful experience that followed a shock that was potentially life-threatening. In these patients, repetition manifests itself in the form of anxiety, various symptoms and repeated dreams, the last of which have the particularity of reproducing the traumatic situation. Consequently, repetition cannot be separated from the transference in psychoanalysis, and what is *repeated* – in general, fragments of repressed traumatic events often dating back to the infantile past – must be *elaborated*.

It is sometimes the case, however, that the process of elaboration in analysis fails, with the result that mere repetition becomes a much more serious *compulsion to repeat* which is liable to compromise therapeutic success. This *compulsion to repeat,* which is opposed to the pleasure/ unpleasure principle, sometimes takes on a literally "demonic" character, as Freud says. In these situations, the repressed infantile experiences that are repeated in the transference do not succeed in being "bound" psychically to the pleasure principle, which makes them "incapable of obeying the secondary process" and for the possibility of elaborating them (1920b, p. 36).

"The aim of all life is death"

Well, then, Freud asks, what could this something that is "beyond" the search for satisfaction – which he had established as the aim of every drive – be like? If the source of the drive is to be found in the organism, is it necessary to look for a more fundamental principle than that of pleasure/unpleasure at the level of living substance? Freud thus ventured outside the psychoanalytic domain proper and put forward a general hypothesis concerning the biological nature of the drives: he suggested that their aim is to re-establish the initial state, that is, the inorganic state before life, for "inanimate things existed before living ones" (1920b, p. 38). Germ-cells seem to escape this process and to oppose the movement of living substance towards death, but their immortality is purely illusory and "and may mean no more than a lengthening of the road that leads to death" (p. 40). From this perspective, then, life may be said to result from a fundamental balance between an inexorable tendency towards death – the death drive – and a tendency towards life represented by the germ-cells which oppose destruction – the life drive or *Eros*.

During the following years, Freud completed his views. Thus, in "The economic problem of masochism" (1924), he considered that the principle of Nirvana is not a state of ideal satisfaction, as he had first presented it, exempt from any physical and psychic pain, but rather expresses a tendency towards the death drive – the peace of cemeteries. This is what differentiates the Nirvana principle from the pleasure principle; a demand of the libido.

Chapter 12

The ego, the id and the superego

Group Psychology and the Analysis of the Ego (1921)

In this essay, Freud asks whether it is possible to transpose at the level of individual psychic space the interactions that can be observed on a grand scale between the group leader and the individuals that make up the group. Up to then, Freud had described the phenomena that unfold within the individual psychic space in terms of their localization, that is, depending on whether they are situated at the conscious, preconscious or unconscious level. His initial approach explained the mechanism of repression, but it was no longer sufficient to account for the many other elements involved in human mental functioning, such as: What is the place of the ego/subject, of the "I"? What is the role of love and hate? What is the effect of "censorship" or "moral conscience"?

The group leader, model for the individual "ego"?

In this essay, taking his theory of the libido as his starting-point, Freud examines what creates and what dissolves the cohesion of a group, or the fascination that a leader exerts. For Freud, neither suggestion nor hypnosis are involved. He shows that only an emotional bond – love – is capable of overcoming both individual narcissisms and the hate that separates the members of a group. He takes as an example the love of Christ in the Church, or the love of the Commander-in Chief in the army. And yet this libidinal tie is not a highly evolved sexual love; it is a primitive form of love whose sexual aims are inhibited and which is called identification: "Identification is known to psychoanalysis as the earliest expression of an emotional tie with another person" (1921, p. 105). Consequently, it is the individual's identification with the leader and the identification of the individuals between themselves that creates the cohesion of a group, and the loss of this emotional tie is the cause of its dissolution, as can be seen in the state of panic.

And yet the tie with the leader is at the same time one that is based on idealisation, so that the individual, fascinated by this figure, sees that his own personality tends to fade into the background to the point that the *ego ideal* represented by the group leader takes the place of the *ego* of each individual. Here Freud takes up again the ideas he had advanced in *Totem and Taboo* (1912–1913) and puts forward the hypothesis that the relations between the group and its leader are a revival of the relations between the sons and the father of the primal horde, and further that, after the murder of the ancestral father, he was replaced by the hero celebrated by the poet's imagination.

The normal and pathological ego ideal

The fact that an idealised person can take possession of the ego of an individual throws light on a variety of clinical situations. Thus in the fascination of love, the idealisation of the object can lead the individual's ego to submit literally to the ideal object, silencing any form of criticism. This is not the case in the normal state of being in love, for the tendency to overestimate the loved object does not lead to a loss of the sense of reality.

Taking as a model the interactions that can be observed between an individual and the leader of the group, Freud transposes them to the inner world of the individual. These interactions, he writes "may be repeated upon this new scene of action within the ego" (p. 130). He also establishes a parallel on the one hand between the tension that exists between the leader of a group and the individuals of which it is composed and, on the other, the tension between the internalised ego ideal, formed by parental demands, and the "ego" of the individual. This inner tension can be exacerbated in pathological cases and even explain the alternations between melancholia and mania.

The Ego and the Id (1923a)

In this synthesis of his hypotheses, Freud clarifies the notion of the "ego" and introduces for the first time those of the "id" and the "superego". This so-called "structural theory" of mental functioning – also called the "second topography" by French psychoanalysts – takes more account of the depth and complexity of the intrapsychic interactions.

The ego

In Freud's work, the notion of "ego" – *das Ich* – takes on different meanings according to the periods. At the outset, the ego designates the personality as a whole: Freud sees it essentially as the locus of what is conscious. From 1923 onwards, with the introduction of the structural theory, Freud presents it as an agency regulating psychic phenomena. On the one hand the *ego* must constantly find a balance between the demands of the *id* – the "reservoir of the drives" – and the imperatives of the *superego*; on the other, the ego manages the relations between the individual and the demands of the external world. Torn between contradictory demands, the personality is the result of the respective forces present and of their dynamic equilibrium. With the introduction of the structural theory, the aim of analysis changed. While the latter had consisted previously of "making conscious that which is unconscious", its aim henceforth was: "Where id was, there shall ego be" (*"Wo Es war, soll Ich werden"* (1933 [1932], p. 80).

The id

A notion borrowed from the psychoanalyst Georg Groddeck, the "id" – *das Es* – constitutes for Freud the great reservoir of the drives and passions. It is governed by the pleasure principle to the detriment of the reality principle. However, unlike Groddeck, Freud does not think that the ego suffers the assaults of the id passively: rather, it seeks to tame them, just as a rider would try to restrain his horse. He writes: ". . . often a rider, if he is not to be parted from his horse, is obliged to guide it where it wants to go; so in the same way, the ego is in the habit of transforming the id's will into action as if it were its own" (1923a, p. 25).

The superego

Henceforth Freud defines the superego – das *Über-Ich* – as an agency that presents itself in relation to the ego as an authority of surveillance.[1] This agency can be benevolent and protective towards the ego, but it can also become critical, and even tyrannical, so that the affective quality of the superego varies according to the individual's personality. The normal function of the superego consists in protecting the ego from being swamped when the pressure from the id is excessive, just as parents must show firmness when a child puts him/herself in danger, for instance by getting too near to a fire or a precipice. During his development, the violence of the child's oedipal impulses decreases, as well as his sense of guilt. He can then overcome the grudging feelings that he has towards his father and his mother and love them in spite of the frustrations that they impose on him. Thanks to the child's gradual identification with his protective parents, his post-oedipal superego allows the ego to tame the incestuous and murderous impulses coming from the id. This is what Freud means when he describes the superego as being the "heir of the Oedipus complex" (1923a, p. 36).

The pathological forms of the superego present very varied affective qualities. In the neuroses, the superego is generally extremely severe towards the ego, even to the point of exerting a sadistic repression of the ego and inhibiting its functioning. This is particularly the case in obsessional neurosis, as exemplified by the Rat Man (see Chapter Nine). In other situations, the superego can be corrupted, leaving the way open for an unleashing of drive impulses, as can be observed in manic states or the perversions. As for the harshness and severity of the superego that can be observed in melancholic depression, Freud attributes the destructive component of it to the action of the death drive: "What is now holding sway in the superego is, as it were, a pure culture of the death instinct, and in fact it often enough succeeds in driving the ego into death, if the latter does not fend off its tyrant in time by the change round into mania" (ibid., p. 53).

The ego and the superego, mosaics of identifications

How are the ego and superego formed? For Freud, these agencies are the result of processes of identification based on the model of the identification with the leader that can be observed in group phenomena. From this point of view, he distinguishes two types of identification, as mentioned earlier (see Chapter Seven). At the beginning of life, it is impossible to distinguish identification from object-cathexis, so that *loving the object* is the equivalent of *being the object.* In other words, early identifications are narcissistic identifications in which the sexual object is introduced into the ego according to the mechanism of melancholic introjection, "which makes it possible to suppose that the character of the ego is a precipitate of abandoned object-cathexes and that it contains the history of those object-choices" (ibid., p. 29).

These first identifications behave as a particular agency in the ego and oppose the ego under the guise of superego or ego ideal. When the ego has become stronger, a more developed form of identification is set up: the ego succeeds in distinguishing love and identification ("I can love the object without confusing myself with it"). It is then able to abandon its sexual aims and to cathect its oedipal objects with a sublimated narcissistic libido, while identifying with traits of their personality. In 1938, Freud summarized the difference between these two processes of identification as follows: "'Having' and 'being' in children. Children like expressing an object-relation by an identification: 'I am the object.' 'Having' is the later of the two; after the loss of the object it relapses into 'being'. Example: the breast. 'The breast is a part of me, I am the breast.' Only later: 'I have it'—that is, 'I am not it' . . ." (1941 [1938], p. 299).

Psychic bisexuality and the Oedipus complex

Freud describes next the relations between the processes of identification and the Oedipus complex. He comes to the conclusion that in its complete form, and taking psychic bisexuality into account, the Oedipus complex has two forms, one direct and one inverted.

In the inverted Oedipus complex, the boy wants to marry his father and eliminate his mother, whom he perceives as a rival. His "passive feminine" wishes in regard to his father lead him, then, to abandon his heterosexual wishes towards his mother. In the girl it is the strength of her first attachment to her mother that leads her to want to be her mother's husband, which inhibits her heterosexual wishes. According to Freud, the two forms of the Oedipus complex coexist in the mind of each individual and, between the male and female tendencies, the proportion varies. From this point of view, the so-called normal psychosexual development of an individual results from the predominance of the direct Oedipus complex over the inverted Oedipus complex.

However, the child's superego is not only formed from the identifications with the parents as ideals; it is also the result of identifications with the parental prohibitions which stood in the way of the fulfilment of incestuous oedipal wishes. In other words, the superego presents "two faces" in its relation to the ego: on the one hand it encourages it – "You *ought to be* like this (like the father)" – but on the other it faces the ego with a prohibition – "You *may not be* like this (like the father)", that is: "You may not do all that he does; some things are his prerogative" (1923a, p. 34). Thus an agency, whose severity varies from one individual to another, becomes detached within the ego: ". . . the more powerful the Oedipus complex was . . . the stricter will be the domination of the superego over the ego later on—in the form of conscience or perhaps of an unconscious sense of guilt" (ibid, pp. 34–35).

The negative therapeutic reaction

Freud compares the ego with a servant who has three masters and is menaced by three dangers, one coming from the external world, the other from the libido of the id, and the third from the severity of the superego. For example, as far as the superego is concerned, we often meet patients who react to making progress in the treatment in a paradoxical manner, for every improvement in their state leads in them to an aggravation of it, a phenomenon Freud calls a "negative therapeutic reaction". What wins through in these patients is not the will to be cured but the need to be ill, because they feel guilty unconsciously and cannot give up the punishment of suffering: "But as far as the patient is concerned this sense of guilt is dumb; it does not tell him he is guilty; he does not feel guilty, he feels ill" (ibid. pp. 49–50). Such a negative therapeutic reaction can be found in the majority of severely neurotic patients; and the sense of guilt is unconscious, compared with the normal sense of guilt which is conscious.

Note

1 To refer to the precursors of the superego, Freud used the following terms at the beginning of his work: the "censor", the "moral conscience" or the "critic of consciousness". In *Group Psychology and the Analysis of the Ego* (1921), he used the term "ego ideal" to refer to the ideal agency that is internalised, without yet speaking of "superego". In 1923, in *The Ego and the Id* (1923a) Freud introduced the term "superego" and, although the notions of ego ideal and superego are equivalent, the use of the term superego prevailed.

Chapter 13

The fear of losing the loved, desired person

In *Inhibitions, Symptoms and Anxiety* (1926 [1925]), Freud discusses a range of subjects from a new angle. I will confine myself to presenting his new views on the origin of anxiety owing to their importance for clinical practice. He attributes a central role to the ego, to the difference with his earlier views, which did not imply this agency: anxiety is henceforth an affect felt by the *ego* when confronted with a danger linked to the fear of being separated from the object and of losing it.[1]

A theory of anxiety replacing the earlier theories

In 1905, Freud had already established a direct link between the appearance of anxiety in the child and the painful feeling of the absence of a loved person. This affirmation was based on the case observation of three-year-old boy who, because he was afraid in the dark, had said to his aunt: "'Auntie speak to me! I'm frightened because it's so dark.' His aunt answered him: 'What good would that do? You can't see me.' 'That doesn't matter,' replied the child, 'if anyone speaks, it gets light'" (1905b, p. 224, note 1).

It was only in 1926 that Freud applied this point of view on the origin of anxiety in the child to the adult. In fact, he had long considered that anxiety in adults was a purely biological phenomenon, an excess of excitation due to unsatisfied libido being transformed directly into anxiety, just as "wine turns to vinegar". He gave as an example the practice of interrupted sexual intercourse. Later, he considered that the anxiety of neurotics could be reduced to a common meaning: the threat of castration. He saw this exemplified in phobic neurotics who have a dominant fear of animals, or in obsessional neurotics for whom the fear of punishment from the superego is dominant.

In 1924, to account for the separation-anxiety that he observed regularly in his patients, Otto Rank published *The Trauma of Birth* (Rank, 1924). For him all crises of anxiety may be considered as repeated attempts to master a primordial trauma, that of birth. Freud was initially in favour of Rank's theory, for he had already affirmed that birth was the first experience of anxiety in the child, but he objected that this initial trauma could not be reproduced in the same way throughout life.

Anxiety, a reaction of the ego to the danger presented by the loss of the object

Stimulated by Rank's book, Freud published *Inhibitions, Symptoms and Anxiety* (1926 [1925]) in which he describes the origin of separation-anxiety as we encounter it in clinical practice. Henceforth, he considered anxiety as an affect experienced by the ego when faced with a danger, which, when one traces it back to its unconscious source, regularly has to do with the fear of separation and the loss of the object. Freud's thesis revolves around the distinction that he makes between the traumatic situation and the situation of danger. The *traumatic* situation submerges the ego and triggers *automatic anxiety*. This is a specific affect, *helplessness* (*Hilflosigkeit*) which is at once a sensation and a feeling of the immature ego that is unable to face the accumulation of excitation coming from the outside or inside, and incapable of mastering it. It is a state of tension that does not reach discharge, but Freud now attributed it to the weakness and helplessness of the individual's ego. In the course of development, when the ego is capable of passing over from the state of passivity to activity, it is able to recognise the situation of *real danger* and to avoid it by releasing *signal-anxiety*. Thanks to this displacement, the reaction of anxiety is reproduced when faced with a danger, this time as an "alarm signal". From a situation of distress that is suffered passively, we move to a situation of actively waiting for it. Other displacements occur thereafter, notably of the danger specifically related to the condition determining the danger, that is, to the loss of the object in its different forms.

The dangers vary according to the different periods of life

The dangers liable to give rise to a traumatic situation vary according to the different periods of life and have the common characteristic of implying separation or the loss of love from an object. Freud states that during normal development each stage corresponds to a condition triggering the anxiety. Developmental progress contributes to eliminating the earlier situation of danger, but these situations can coexist in one and the same individual and come into play simultaneously.

The danger of birth

At this stage the anxiety felt by the newborn and the infant as a danger is solely the result of a state of helplessness, without it being necessary to introduce the separation with the mother. Indeed, for Freud, the newborn and the infant do not yet perceive the mother as a separate and different person. That is why the first anxiety corresponds to a fear of annihilation rather than to the fear of separation proper. At a later stage, when the infant is capable of perceiving his mother as an object, the situation of danger shifts from distress to fear of separation and loss of the object: "When the infant has found out by experience that an external, perceptible object can put an end to the dangerous situation which is reminiscent of birth, the content of the danger it fears is displaced from the economic situation on to the condition which determined the situation, viz., the loss of object. It is the absence of the mother that is now the danger; and as soon as that danger arises the infant gives the signal of anxiety, before the dreaded economic situation has set in" (1926 [1925], p. 138).

The loss of the mother as object

Later on, the infant begins to perceive the presence of his mother, but cannot as yet distinguish temporary absence from lasting loss: "As soon as it loses sight of its mother it behaves as if he were never going to see her again" (1926 [1925], p. 169). Then, the child moves progressively from fear of losing the object to the fear of losing the object's love.

Castration anxiety as the danger of object loss

This danger occurs during the phallic stage. It is also a form of separation-anxiety determined by the loss of the object, but the helplessness is caused by a "special need", genital libido. It is worth recalling here that Freud reserves the term castration explicitly for the loss of the penis in order to avoid using the term castration for the loss of the mother's breast, the loss of faeces, or the separation of birth, as psychoanalysts were beginning to do: "While recognizing all of these roots of the complex, I have nevertheless put forward the view that the term 'castration complex' ought to be confined to those excitations and consequences which are bound up with the loss of the *penis*" (1909a, p. 8, note 2, added 1923).

The danger of losing the love of the superego

With developmental progress, the infant, who first attributes castration-anxiety to an internalized parental agency, gradually attributes it to a more impersonal agency so that castration-anxiety turns into moral anxiety. For the ego the danger then lies in the fear of losing the love of the superego and it responds with signal anxiety. The ultimate form of anxiety in relation to the superego would be death anxiety, that is, anxiety projected into the powers of destiny.

Separation-anxieties and psychoanalytic process

By introducing different levels of anxiety into the course of infantile development, Freud threw fresh light on the relationship between the two main types of anxiety that we meet with in the psychoanalytic treatment: on the one hand, separation-anxiety, which is characteristic of the pregenital stages and, on the other, castration anxiety, which is characteristic of the Oedipus complex. One of the aims of psychoanalytic work consists in helping the analysand to elaborate the early separation-anxieties that are characteristic of the pregenital level so that he can gradually cope with elaborating the anxieties linked to the oedipal situation, which are characteristic of the genital level. In *Inhibitions, Symptoms and Anxiety*, Freud also sheds new light on the origin of defences, no doubt brought into play by the separation-anxieties that can be observed at the end of sessions or with breaks due to weekends and holidays. He also gives up the idea according to which repression is at the origin of anxiety. Henceforth, he asserts that it is the ego that produces symptoms and defences with the aim of avoiding the emergence of anxiety, which, in the last analysis, is regularly the unconscious fear of separation and of the loss of the loved and desired object.

The ideas advanced by Freud in *Inhibitions, Symptoms and Anxiety* have sometimes been considered as pure theoretical speculation, especially as he gives few examples drawn from his practice. And yet I think that these phenomena, which psychoanalysts encounter daily in their clinical work, certainly drew Freud's attention (Quinodoz, 1991).

Note

1 On the psychoanalytic use of the term "object", see Chapter Six, note 1.

Chapter 14

Psychosis, disavowal of reality and splitting of the ego

Throughout his work, Freud sought to highlight the specific mechanisms of psychosis and to establish the differences between neurosis and psychosis. He tackled the question from different angles. For example, he devoted a detailed study to the paranoiac persecution mania and hallucinations of President Schreber (Freud, 1911). In the case of the "Wolf Man" (1918 [1914]), we can see that Freud put the emphasis mainly on the neurotic aspects, and that these coexisted with psychotic aspects that would be analysed subsequently by Ruth Mack Brunswick.

The language of the schizophrenic

Freud was also concerned to study the particular language of the schizophrenic. In "The Unconscious" (1915c), he shows that the unconscious reveals itself better in a psychotic patient than in neurosis, owing to the absence of the obstacle created by repression. He notes that schizophrenics present a particular alteration of language and that their words are subject to a mechanism of condensation similar to the primary process that produces images in dreams. *Words* become equivalent to the *things* or *acts* that they designate.

For example, Freud cites the case of one of the patients of his disciple Victor Tausk, who was disturbed by the idea that there were "holes" in his socks. Indeed, the word "hole" had become for him a source of terror because it combined two meanings, the hole in his socks and the opening of a woman's genitals. With this example, we can see that a schizophrenic patient reveals without detours or resistance the unconscious symbolic meaning of his inhibition, for the preconscious does not play for him its mediating role between unconscious and conscious. In neurosis, the preconscious system intervenes in the process of repression. The primitive symbolism that characterises the language of schizophrenics falls within the distinction established by Freud between, on the one hand, the primary processes that predominate in psychosis and, on the other, the secondary processes that predominate in neurosis and which are characterised by symbolic representation. From this point of view, the psychoanalytic treatment may be considered as consisting in distinguishing words from acts, in differentiating *thinking* from *acting,* in order to allow secondary processes to prevail over primary processes.

Disavowal of reality and splitting of the ego

According to Freud the disavowal of reality is the specific mode of psychosis. This mechanism consists in refusing unconsciously to see a reality that is unbearable and traumatising for the ego. He also regards it as a characteristic of perversion ("Fetishism", 1927b). Its consequence is that it causes a splitting of the ego, that is, a division within it. This disavowal never affects the whole of the ego but a certain proportion of it which varies, with the result that a part of the ego recognises reality, while the other rejects it. From the psychopathological point of view, there is a great difference between the mechanism of repression, which does not alter the structure of the ego, and splitting, which divides the ego. Owing to this division, the ego is inhabited by a contradictory attitude due to the fact that one part of the ego accepts reality while another part rejects it.

Freud notes this splitting first in pathological mourning, where the ego of the depressive is "split" between a part that recognises the loss of the loved object or ideal and a part that denies it. He cites the example of a young man who had "scotomized" – just as a blind spot would do – the death of his father. Two positions existed within him: one according to which his father was still living; the other according to which he was dead. In the case of fetishism, Freud notes that two contradictory attitudes are also at work: one part of the ego recognises the absence of the penis in women, while the other disavows this reality and imagines that the fetish is a substitute for the penis in women (Freud, 1927b).

Splitting of the ego, also in neurosis

Freud goes further and henceforth asserts that splitting of the ego exists not only in psychosis or other states, such as fetishism, but also in neurosis: "The view which postulates that in all psychoses there is a *splitting of the ego* could not call for so much notice if it did not turn out to apply to other states more like the neuroses and, finally, to the neuroses themselves (1940, p. 202). Freud concludes that psychic normality or pathology is the result of a balance of forces between two contrary attitudes that are independent of each other, one accepting reality, the other rejecting it: "The disavowal is always supplemented by an acknowledgement; two contrary and independent attitudes always arise and result in the situation of there being a splitting of the ego. Once more the issue depends on which of the two can seize hold of the greater intensity" (ibid., p. 204). He concludes by repeating how difficult it is to perceive the existence of these psychic phenomena: "In conclusion, it is only necessary to point out how little of all these processes becomes known to us through our conscious perception" (ibid., p. 204).

Chapter 15

Religion and civilization

Pessimism or lucidity?

Freud applied his discoveries to other domains than that of psychoanalysis. For example, he studied from a psychoanalytic point of view the life and work of artists such as Leonardo da Vinci, Michelangelo and Dostoevsky, or figures like Moses. He also tackled questions concerning human society in general, notably in two works that had a great impact, *The Future of an Illusion* (1927a) and *Civilization and its Discontents* (1930).

The Future of an Illusion (1927a)

High moral values to protect civilization

In *The Future of an Illusion,* Freud begins by showing how civilization, in order to protect itself from the destructive tendencies of the individuals that compose it, must possess high moral values. Among them, he includes values of a psychological order, cultural ideals, and also religious ideas, the latter of which constitute in his view the most important moral value for the preservation of civilization. He pursues this essay in the form of a dialogue with an imaginary "adversary", in whom one of his correspondents, the Lutheran pastor, Oskar Pfister, from Zurich, has been recognised. With respect to religion, he says that the only model he is taking as a reference point is Christianity, as it is practised in the West.

Where do religious ideas come from?

To show that the idea of God is formed on a strictly profane basis and anchored in individual psychology, Freud draws on the recent contributions of psychoanalysis. He refers in the first place to the notion of "infantile helplessness" as a factor triggering anxiety,[1] a notion that he introduced in 1926 in *Inhibitions, Symptoms and Anxiety* (see Chapter Thirteen). For him, the distress of the human being faced with the danger of existence and with the enigma of death is identical to the physical and psychological helplessness of the young child fearing separation from, and loss of, the people around him whom he loves. Just as distress leads the young child to seek help from his mother first, and then from his father, so the human being has recourse to a "benevolent Providence"; in this way life after death is seen as a continuation of our earthly life, providing perfection and an ideal. Thus, in Freud's view the idea of God is formed on the model both of infantile helplessness and on that of the relationship to the father.

Religious ideas are illusions

Taking the view that religious ideas are based on evidence that is not very solid, in spite of their considerable influence, Freud asserts that they are illusions and constitute the fulfilment of the deepest and most powerful wishes of humanity. Freud adds that he is neither for or against "the truth-value of religious doctrines" (1927a, p.33), but is surprised that the idea of God the creator, a God of Providence, of a moral order of the universe and of a future life, coincides not only with our own wishes but also with those of our primal ancestors.

A profession of faith in science

Responding to the objections raised by his interlocutor, Freud defends himself against the charge of being a dreamer and of allowing himself to be carried away by his own illusions. On the contrary, he places great hope in the primacy of intelligence and of the scientific spirit, even if their reign is still far from accomplished. He reiterates his confidence in science which is constantly developing and concludes: "No, our science is no illusion. But an illusion it would be to suppose that what science cannot give us we can get elsewhere" (ibid., p. 56). In his last work, *Moses and Monotheism* (1939), Freud notes that the idea of God in the religion of Moses is much more sublime than in the others. Nevertheless he repeats that he does not believe in the existence of a single God. For him, this belief stems from the idea that a single figure really existed in primitive times and that he was raised above the others to the rank of a divinity. Thereafter, the historical existence of this man was forgotten. But the idea of a single God reappeared in humanity in the same way as the return of the repressed in the neurotic.

Controversial questions

The publication of *The Future of an Illusion* gave rise immediately to controversies that are far from being resolved. The first to protest was the pastor Oskar Pfister: the interest of his debate with Freud lies in the fact that their reciprocal arguments already contain the main themes of the subsequent debates. Thus, Pfister reproaches Freud for focusing solely on the pathological aspects of religious practice and not on the phenomenon of religion as a whole. Freud opposes psychoanalysis to religion, while Pfister sees psychoanalysis as a possibility for the believer to cleanse his faith. This was also the position taken later by Paul Ricoeur (1965) who spoke out against the prejudice that claims that psychoanalysis is iconoclastic. According to him, a "demolition" of religion can very well be the critical expression of a faith cleansed of all idolatry. As for the Roman Catholic Church, notwithstanding its reservations, it has never pronounced an official condemnation of psychoanalysis.

For my part, I think that Freud's position was coloured by a purely rational psychological perspective and that he did not take into account the spiritual dimension implied by religious faith, particularly in the Christian version. For me, psychoanalysis and religious faith each occupy their own specific field. However, given their inevitable inter-actions, it is important, I think, to distinguish one field from the other so that the existence of one does not impede the existence of the other. It is a matter of distinguishing between them so as not to confuse them.

Civilization and its Discontents (1930)

Written at the time of the Great Depression of 1930 and of the rise of Nazism in Germany, this book is often seen as a dark but lucid sociological testament. Freud begins by offering a bold synthesis which highlights the precarious equilibrium of the human being in a civilization which is supposed to protect him, but paradoxically risks destroying him. This equilibrium is simply the reflection of the fundamental conflict between the life drive and the death drive, to which Freud lent increasing credence (see Chapter Eleven).

Owing to the fact that civilization restricts the sexual and aggressive instincts of individuals with the aim of maintaining the cohesion of society, civilization comes into conflict with its members, taken individually, who, if they rebel, can destroy it. However, and this is the point Freud is making, the conflict that exists in external reality between individuals and civilization has its counterpart in the conflict that is played out within the psyche of each person, namely, between the demands of the superego – now feared as was external authority before – and the ego – which represents the interests of the individual. For Freud, the unconscious sense of guilt that results from this unconscious conflict is at the origin of "the discontents of civilization". It accounts for the precarious nature of the human condition, subject as it is to the uncertainties of the conflict between the life drive and the death drive by which it is inhabited, as well as to its own illusions. The rather pessimistic note on which the work concludes, in particular when Freud raises questions as to the future of humanity in view of the fact that with the help of technology men have acquired the means of exterminating one another to the last man, would soon prove him right.

Note

1 See Chapter Sixteen, note 8.

Chapter 16

Sigmund Freud from 1900 to 1939[1]

1900. Freud was forty-four years of age, and had just published *The Interpretation of Dreams* (1900). **1901**. He broke off relations with Wilhelm Fliess. During the next five years, he devoted three works to the development of his innovative ideas: *The Psychopathology of Everyday Life* (1901b) had the aim of demonstrating to the public at large the existence of the unconscious through parapraxes and bungled actions; *Jokes and their Relation with the Unconscious* (1905a) established the proximity of the *Witz* with the mechanisms at the basis of dream-formation; *Three Essays on the Theory of Sexuality* (1905b) revolutionised existing prejudices about infantile and adult sexuality. This last work shocked the public and scientific circles. **1902**. Foundation of the *Psychological Wednesday Society,* where his close followers met to discuss his work. Otto Rank, from Vienna, became its secretary in 1905, at the age of twenty two. **1903**. Freud received the title of "Professor Extraordinary". **1905**. He published *Fragment of an Analysis of a Case of Hysteria* (1905c), an account of the discovery of the transference which Freud had not noticed before the patient broke off her analysis prematurely, confusing Freud unconsciously with her father, a seducer. Gradually, Freud emerged from his "splendid isolation" and his ideas began to be recognised at an international level.

1907. In Vienna, he received a visit from those who were to become his first disciples: Max Eitingon, Carl Gustav Jung and Karl Abraham, all three assistants of Professor Eugen Bleuler, Director of the Burghölzi

Clinic in Zurich. **1908**. Sándor Ferenczi (Budapest) and Ernest Jones (London) followed. In the same year the first International Congress of Psychoanalysis was held in Salzburg, where Freud presented the case of the "Rat Man" (1909b). **1909**. He published "Analysis of a phobia in a five-year-old boy" (1909a), the first child analysis, conducted with his father, Max Graf, and supervised by Freud. The Vienna Psychoanalytic Society was officially founded. Freud began a correspondence with Pastor Oskar Pfister from Zurich, an exchange that would continue until 1939. Freud was invited by G. Stanley Hall to give a series of lectures at Clark University in Worcester (United States), and was accompanied by Ferenczi and Jung. **1910**. On Ferenczi's initiative, the *International Psychoanalytical Association* (IPA) was founded. Jung became its first president. Freud published "Psycho-analytic notes on an autobiographical account of a case of paranoia' (Dementia paranoides)" (1911), then *Totem and Taboo* (1912–1913). Conflicts arose between the first psychoanalysts. Adler and Wilhelm Stekel distanced themselves from Freud's group. A "Secret Committee" was created around Freud to promote cohesion between his pupils within the psychoanalytic movement. He met Lou Andreas Salomé, a prominent figure in literary circles.

1912. After being considered as Freud's heir apparent, Jung separated from him, due mainly to divergent opinions on the place of sexuality, particularly in the psychoses. The First World War broke out: Martin and Ernst, two of Freud's sons, were mobilised. **1914–1916**. Ferenczi did three short analyses with Freud. In 1915, Freud published his *Papers on Metapsychology,* a synthesis of his theoretical views. His son, Olivier, was mobilised. Freud was experiencing a period of isolation and material privation. Psychoanalysis showed its usefulness in the treatment of the "war neuroses" and post-traumatic neuroses. The psychoanalytic treatment of manic depressive patients by Karl Abraham inspired Freud to write "Mourning and melancholia" (1917b). **1918**. The "Wolf Man" (1918 [1914]) was published the year the war ended. Anna Freud did her first analysis with her own father. **1919**. Viktor Tausk, a close disciple of Freud, committed suicide. Freud's benefactor, Anton von Freund, died. **1920**. Sophie, one of Freud's daughters, died from Spanish influenza. Ernest Jones founded

✤

the *International Journal of Psychoanalysis*. Freud published *Beyond the Pleasure Principle* (1920b), which postulated the existence of a fundamental conflict between the life- instincts and the death-instinct, a hypothesis which has long been contested by psychoanalysts themselves. Increasingly recognised at the international level, Freud devoted himself to the analysis of his colleagues who came to him from all over the world, and particularly from North America. **1921.** In *Group Psychology and the Analysis of the Ego* (1921), he compared the phenomenon of identification with the leader of a group with the identification with parents that is constitutive of the individual ego. **1923**. Freud published *The Ego and the Id* (1923a), in which he introduced the concept of the superego and proposed an innovative psychic organisation centred on the relations between the ego, the id, and the superego. Freud was suffering from cancer of the jaw which led to a series of incapacitating and painful surgical interventions during the last sixteen years of his life. **1924**. Anna undertook a second period of analysis with her father. **1925**. Karl Abraham died, as well as Josef Breuer. Freud celebrated his seventieth birthday. Otto Rank and Sandor Ferenczi began to distance themselves from Freud. These two disciples proposed modifications to psychoanalytic practice by centering it on the present of the relationship. **1926**. Melanie Klein arrived in London on the invitation of Jones. In *Inhibitions, Symptoms and Anxiety* (1926 [1925]), Freud now considered that the origin of anxiety was linked to the fear of loss and of separation with a loved, desired person. **1927**. *The Future of an Illusion* (1927a) was an opportunity for Freud to affirm his faith in science and to consider that religions are the result of an illusory projection that is purely psychological. The Tenth International Congress of Psychoanalysis was held in Innsbruck. **1929**. The world entered the Great Depression. **1930**. Amalia, Freud's mother, died at the age of ninety-five. Freud received the Goethe prize for the literary quality of his writing. Published at the time of the Great Depression, *Civilization and its Discontents* (1930) broached the question of human misery from a pessimistic angle. Nazism and anti-Semitism were on the rise in Germany and Austria. **1932**. The Twelfth International Congress of Psychoanalysis was held in Wiesbaden. **1933**. Adolf Hitler came to power. Freud's works were burned in public. Ferenczi died. Freud published his *New Introductory Lectures on Psychoanalysis* (1933 [1932]). Freud threw himself into a series of studies on psychosis and perversions. **1936**. Freud celebrated his eightieth birthday. The same year, he met Romain Rolland. **1937**. Lou Andreas Salomé died. Freud published "Analysis terminable and interminable" (1937), and then "Constructions in analysis" (1937). **1938**. With the help of Marie Bonaparte, Ernest Jones, and the ambassador of the United States, William C. Bullitt, Freud agreed to leave Vienna for London, accompanied, among others, by his wife Martha and their daughter Anna. **1939**. Freud published *Moses and Monotheism* (1939), before dying in London on 23 September, at the age of eighty three.

Note

1 For the period from 1856 to 1900, see Chapter One.

Bibliography

Freud, S. with J. Breuer (1895). *Studies on Hysteria. S.E.* **2**.

Freud, S. (1887–1904). *The Complete Letters of Sigmund Freud to Wilhelm Fliess, 1887–1904*, trans. & ed. J.M. Masson. Cambridge, MA & London: Harvard University Press, 1985.

Freud, S. (1900). *The Interpretation of Dreams. S.E.* **4 & 5**.

Freud, S. (1901a). *On Dreams. S.E.* **5**: 633–686.

Freud, S. (1901b). *The Psychopathology of Everyday Life. S.E.* **6**: 1–278.

Freud, S. (1905a). *Jokes and their Relation to the Unconscious. S.E.* **8**: 9–236.

Freud, S. (1905b). *Three Essays on the Theory of Sexuality. S.E.* **7**: 123–243.

Freud, S. (1905c [1901]). Fragment of an analysis of a case of hysteria. *S.E.* **7**: 7–122.

Freud, S. (1909a). Analysis of a phobia in a five-year-old boy. *S.E.* **10**: 5–149.

Freud, S. (1909b). Notes upon a case of obsessional neurosis. *S.E.* **10**: 255–318.

Freud, S. (1911 [1910]). Psychoanalytic notes on an autobiographical account of a case of paranoia (Dementia paranoides). *S.E.* **12**: 1–82.

Freud, S. (1912–1913). *Totem and Taboo. S.E.* **13**: 1–161.

Freud, S. (1912). Recommendations to physicians practising psycho-analysis. *S.E.* **12:** 111–120.

Freud, S. (1914). Remembering, repeating and working-through. *S.E.* **12**: 145–156.

Freud, S. (1915a) Instincts and their vicissitudes. *S.E.* **14**: 109–140.

Freud, S. (1915b). Repression. *S.E.* **14**: 141–158.

Freud, S. (1915c).The unconscious. *S.E.* **14**: 166–215.

Freud, S. (1917a). A metapsychological supplement to the theory of dreams. *S.E.* **14:** 222–235.

Freud, S. (1917b). Mourning and melancholia. *S.E.* **14**: 237–260.

Freud, S. (1918 [1914]). From the history of an infantile neurosis. *S.E.* **17**: 1–122.

Freud, S. (1919). A child is being beaten. *S.E.* **17**: 179–204.

Freud, S. (1920a). The psychogenesis of a case of homosexuality in a woman. *S.E.* **18**: 147–172.

Freud, S. (1920b). *Beyond the Pleasure Principle. S.E.* **18**:1–64.

Freud, S. (1921). *Group Psychology and the Analysis of the Ego. S.E.* **18**: 65–143.

Freud, S. (1923a). *The Ego and the Id. S.E.* **19**: 3–66.

Freud, S. (1923b). The infantile genital organisation. *S.E.* **19**: 141–145.

Freud, S. (1924). The economic problem of masochism. *S.E.* **19**: 15–70.

Freud, S. (1926 [1925]). *Inhibitions, Symptoms and Anxiety. S.E.* **20**: 75–174.

Freud, S. (1927a). *The Future of an Illusion. S.E.* **21**: 1–56.

Freud, S. (1927b). Fetishism. *S.E.* **21**: 147–158.

Freud S (1930). *Civilization and its Discontents. S.E.* **21**: 57–146.

Freud, S. (1933 [1932]). *New Introductory Lectures on Psychoanalysis. S.E.* **22**: 1–182.

Freud, S. (1937). Analysis terminable and interminable. *S.E.* **23**: 209–253.

Freud, S. (1939). *Moses and Monotheism. S.E.* **23**: 1–137.

Freud, S. (1940). *An Outline of Psychoanalysis. S.E.* **23**: 139–208.

Freud, S. (1941 [1938]). Findings, ideas, problems. *S.E.* **23**: 299–300.

Freud, S. (1950 [1895]). *Project for a Scientific Psychology. S.E.* **1**: 281–397.

Freud, S. (1987). *A Phylogenetic Fantasy: Overview of the Transference Neuroses.* Harvard University Press.

Laplanche, J. & Pontalis, J.-B. (1967). *The Language of Psychoanalysis*, trans. D. Nicholson-Smith. London: Hogarth, 1973.

Quinodoz, J.-M. (1991). *The Taming of Solitude: Separation Anxiety in Psychoanalysis,* trans. Ph. Slotkin. London & New York: Routledge, 1993.

Quinodoz, D. (2002). *Words That Touch: A Psychoanalyst Learns to Speak,* trans. Ph. Slotkin. London: Karnac, 2003.

Rank, O. (1924). *The Trauma of Birth.* London: Routledge & Kegan Paul.

Ricoeur, P. (1965). *Freud and Philosophy: An Essay on Interpretation*, trans. D. Savage. New Haven: Yale University Press, 1970.

Schreber, D.P. (1903). *Memoirs of my Nervous Illness*, trans. I. Macalpine, & R. Hunter. London: Dawson & Sons, 1955.

Index